EFFECTIVE MANAGEMENT IN PRIMARY SCHOOLS

EFFECTIVE MANAGEMENT IN PRIMARY SCHOOLS

Alan and Audrey Paisey

Basil Blackwell

To Norah
and
our many friends and colleagues in primary education

Published by Basil Blackwell Ltd
108 Cowley Road
Oxford OX4 1JF
England

British Library Cataloguing in Publication Data

Paisey, Alan
    Effective management in primary schools.
    1. Elementary schools – Great Britain – Administration
    I. Title   II. Paisey, Audrey
    372.12′00941   LB2822.5

ISBN 0-631-15325-X

Typeset in 10 pt Sabon
by MULTIPLEX techniques ltd, St Mary Cray, Kent.
Printed in Great Britain by T.J. Press Ltd, Cornwall

Contents

List of figures

Preface

The increase of public interest in education, crystallised by a range of Acts of Parliament on education — notably those of 1980, 1981, 1986 and 1988 — has led to greater demands on the managerial* capacity of the Head and other staff in the primary school. These demands are felt particularly over the design and development of the curriculum, the projection of the school's public image, the recruitment of pupils and the ways and means needed to govern and resource the school.

This book, therefore, is primarily intended for Heads of primary schools, but it is hoped that deputy heads and other senior staff will also find it useful along their own path to headship. School governors and others whose work takes them in and out of schools and who need to understand the work of headteachers may, in addition, find this book of interest.

Education in primary schools today is kaleidoscopic in nature. It makes wide and varied demands on the Head and teaching staff. All concerned need to keep in mind not only the rate and range of changes which affect primary schools, but also the central and unchanging task of the school — to obtain the educational development of every child by all possible means, with a constant attitude of goodwill towards each.

Effective Management in Primary Schools is offered in support of Heads in this complex task. Its theme is the effective accomplishment of the task. Illustrative material in the text has been gathered specifically for this purpose. Most of the research data have been gathered direct from Heads and other senior staff.

Many Heads in the primary sector are now being offered non-award-bearing management training courses, under the auspices of local education authorities or the Department of Education and Science. In some cases Heads themselves engage in the training function as full-time or part-time tutors. The contents of this book may be of use to those concerned with such courses, whether as course members or as tutors. In addition, a model of one such management course is included as an Appendix to the main text of the book. Developed in practice over a five year period and subjected to regular evaluation and fine tuning, it has been used for the Department of Education and Science 20 Day Management Course, based at La Sainte Union College of Higher Education, Southampton, from 1985 to 1987, for primary school Heads in the region.

We wish to express our thanks to the many Heads, deputy heads and other staff who have helped in the making of this book, in one way or another. This applies particularly to the development of the Head's management performance profile in Chapter 10. Reference numbers found in the text refer to the notes on p 176.

We acknowledge with gratitude the permission given by the following to use their material in this book: David Picton-Jones (p 7); Blackmore Vale Publishing (p 91); The Falmer Press (pp 94-95); Tom Simpson (pp 96-98); Department of Education and Science / HMSO (p 104); International Labour Office (pp 105-106); Lawrence Cameron (p 125); Christopher Watts (pp 131-132); Frank Agness (p 138); L.G. Cameron/ University of Ulster (pp 150-151); Derek Waters (p 152).

Alan and Audrey Paisey
Berwick St John, Wiltshire

---

* The words 'management' and 'managerial' – as in management task or managerial skills – are used interchangeably.

1

Being alert to the management task

The Head is the primary school's general manager. This is as true of the Head of a small village school as it is of the Head of a large urban or suburban school, even though the former may need to contribute a full teaching week and the latter may not need to teach at all. In the pivotal position of general manager, the responsibility of the Head is to know and to understand all aspects of the life and work of the school and to give the school leadership.

This chapter presents a framework of reference for the Head's task and some guidelines on how to approach it. Its purpose is to indicate the full scope of the general management responsibility, since the first step towards effective management is being alert to what the task involves. Becoming Head of a primary school is an unprecedented event in the professional life of a teacher. It is different from all other posts previously held. This is not only because of the assumption of the title, status and salary of headship but also because of the unique human feelings and experience involved.

The uniqueness of becoming Head is particularly marked in the primary school since posts previously held — up to and including deputy headship — do not provide general management experience in the normal course of events. Most primary schools are too small to warrant the cost of having a non-teaching deputy head with time to carry out general management duties. Some Heads make a special effort to give their deputies general management experience as professional training for headship; other Heads do so to relieve the pressure on themselves. But many Heads provide no such experience, leaving their deputies ignorant of the general management of the school in allowing them to take on little responsibility beyond their own class teaching duties.

Whatever the degree of help and encouragement a teacher may have received from other Heads on the way, it is still a singular experience for that teacher to be appointed to his or her own headship. Headship introduces a new order of risk. It exposes the incumbent to a new measure of visibility, scrutiny, comment and judgement.

The general management task calls for increased and possibly untested intellectual, emotional and interpersonal strengths and skills. Above all, it involves learning to live with ultimate responsibility, which even an acting Head does not carry or experience. This is the Head's duty, legally framed in the school's *Articles of Government*: that he or she 'shall control the internal organisation, managment and discipline' of the school and 'shall exercise supervision over the teaching and non-teaching staff'.

Following the natural elation at being appointed to a headship, the teacher may find that a variety of psychological and practical issues emerge, as these examples show:

In the school where I was deputy head before coming here as Head, I was given every opportunity to spread my wings and get experience in all sorts of things. Even so, now I am Head myself it all feels different — there is a tremendous feeling of infinity about everything.

I was a bit old to be appointed as Head at forty-four, and surprised, too, since it was my very first application. I had to get along with a deputy head who had not applied for the headship but was extremely competent. What has struck me most about it all is how tired I have been. I have felt stretched in all directions at once.

There was no job description. I felt alone and with a sense of isolation. Suddenly there were no parameters to my professional life. The switch from teaching to headship was far more severe than I had imagined. I think the lack of administrative training affected me the most. The amount and tediousness of the administrative work caused me a lot of stress.

It was the range of concerns which came as a shock to me. I found myself taking each new concern home to my family. My wife ended up by saying each time "Oh, not that school again".

As a deputy head I had always expected my Head to teach. I thought I had a pretty good idea how a school should be run. Now I suddenly find myself redundant in the sense that I do not know the answers to questions as the new Head of this school. The deputy head here expects me to teach but I am trying desperately to get to grips with understanding the school first. This is a different reality. I am reflecting how tolerant and able my previous Head must have been when I was his deputy.

Many deputy heads are too inflated; I was myself. I often wanted something done without seeing all the consequences. Being Head, I have found it necessary to study the ripple effect because almost everything that happens affects many other things.

The meaning of management

The term 'general management' is used to indicate the task of the Head; it implies that others are engaged in specific management tasks. The Head has the inclusive job of presiding over all that is happening in the school organisation. But everybody is engaged in managing; the difference lies in the level at which they manage. Every teacher is managing children, physical resources, space, time and often other staff; but at a limited level of importance, in that their work usually concerns only part of the organisation and may not affect the whole. The Head's management task, by contrast, is meant to affect the whole school. If it is insignificant in stature and fails to affect the whole school, it is deemed to be inadequate management.

The reservations which some teachers express about management, as in the following examples, are often based on a misunderstanding of the nature of management:

Management isn't to do with education, is it?

It can be good for the school, can't it?

It's all right up to a point, but we ought not to have too much of it.

I've never been quite sure whether we should have it or not in primary schools — I suppose it is all right in secondary schools.

We shall have to look out when the new Head arrives — he's into this management thing you know.

It is a pity that such misconceptions of management exist in teaching. As far as the primary school is concerned, management, as in organisations everywhere, is necessary and neutral. In essence, *management is human behaviour purposefully directed for the good of the organisation.* It is not something an organisation can choose to have or not have, like buying or not buying a particular set of books or a new overhead projector. Management is inescapable and ubiquitous; it exists because diverse human beings have to work together in organisations. The way in which people with managerial responsibility behave towards others gives management as a human necessity a good or bad name. Heads of primary schools have always had to manage. They have done so well or badly. Only the form which management takes can be in dispute, not the need for management. Everybody wants good management in school; nobody wants bad management.

Those who have had the experience of bad or ineffectual management may be rightly resentful but this feeling should not cloud their expectations of good management and the desire to work for its achievement. Some teachers have been brought up to have an antipathy to 'the management' – as opposed to 'the men' or 'the workers' – which may be ideologically based and difficult to overcome. On attaining headship, it can handicap a teacher in coming to terms with himself or herself and the job in hand.

In the primary school, management is the process of marshalling and combining resources of all kinds in sufficient quantity and of sufficient quality to ensure that set objectives are reached. If the management is performed well, especially good results will be achieved. If the general circumstances at the time happen to be difficult or unpropitious, then the management can be judged particularly meritorious.

Management is human intellectual and physical activity linking resources and objectives

Effective management is getting exceptional results from unexceptional resources — especially when carried out in unpropitious circumstances

In practice, this process takes the form of a series of functions familiar to managers everywhere. These include:
1   planning
2   organising
3   communicating
4   directing
5   staffing
6   motivating
7   coordinating
8   reporting
9   budgeting
10   evaluating

For the Head of the primary school the general management task constitutes a new dimension of professionalism, taking precedence over that of teaching. If all goes well, it should be a pleasurable experience. It is bound to involve hard work. Sometimes it will resemble a battle and be very costly in personal wear and tear. Management becomes a nightmare for some and can cause ill-health or at least constant worry and unhappiness. It need not do so. There is a great deal of know-how in management which needs to be made as accessible as possible to all those in senior positions in primary schools.

A career in management is like a career in teaching. It can become more effective and personally tolerable as a result of assiduous application and experience. But it helps to have as much prior knowledge as possible and to enrich that knowledge constantly whilst in post.

One Head's approach to the task

The Head cannot accomplish the task of general management without viewing and understanding the school as an inclusive whole, and doing so clearly and steadily. The complexity of school life is such that it is relatively easy to become preoccupied or sidetracked by a part or parts of it, whereas general management requires a sustained whole view. To maintain this needs systematic effort — not only prior to and during the early stages of appointment, but also in subsequent years; not to do so is an abdication of duty.

The Head is in the very best position to have an inclusive overview of the school. He or she is appointed for that very purpose. Many other individuals and whole groups will also have their own overview of the school but this, by definition, cannot be as complete as that of the Head. Their overviews are necessary to the Head in building up his or her own inclusive view of the school. These other individuals may, however, make little effort to understand the wider needs and issues of the school. One newly appointed Head, reflecting on his first year of headship, commented:

I came to the conclusion that a whole-school perspective on curricular and pastoral issues was notably lacking; staff were concerned with narrow self-interest and quarrels over status and prerogatives. Something had to be done about it.

If the Head is unable to develop an inclusive overview – that is, to grasp the whole school situation and to increase his or her understanding of it — the school has a serious disability. To acquire an inclusive overview takes some intellectual effort and time. Towards this end, it is helpful to have a model or framework of reference for organising knowledge and understanding in the mind. This can aid clarity of communication and action in the process of managing the school and promoting self-confidence, as illustrated in the following case study.

The teacher in this case found himself at the end of the summer term as deputy head in one school and six weeks later, at the beginning of the next term, as Head of another. His experience was not uncommon in promotions to headships in primary schools, in that he had no contact during the working day with the school to which he had been appointed, until the first day of the new term itself. No invitations were given for him to visit the school during the previous term and he sought none.

On taking up his first headship, he experienced a stressful period of 'learning by doing' — literally undergoing instant headship. The many people involved — the school's governors, staff and local education authority officers and advisers — apparently assumed or accepted that the accession to headship could take place in this way. Justification for this lies in the belief that a teacher's antecedent experiences in the teaching profession are developmental and suitable as preparation for headship generally. But it all depends on what headship implies. Too often headship is thought of in terms of expertise limited to keeping things going — dealing successfully with the plethora of events, varied though they may be, which make up the busy working day of the primary school and are dealt with only and as they occur. If teachers are bred on such expectations, it is too late when they are Heads to expect them to be versed in the management of innovative intervention, to be used to strategic thinking and to be able to exercise greater managerial autonomy at school level as increased powers are afforded them.

Three years later this Head applied for and obtained the headship of a much larger school. Armed with the experience of finding out that lack of personal preparation had led to difficulty and anxiety in his first headship, he determined to tackle his new job in a more constructive way. He made a model of his own observations and the information that came his way unsolicited, or which he purposely sought. He noted, recorded and classified these data, incidentally monitoring the development of his own understanding as he did so.

His preparatory work for the new headship fell into two phases — one covering the term up to his arrival in post, the other the first half of term after arriving in post. He constructed an initial management model with five categories. These concerned matters relating to:

- curriculum
- external relations
- problems
- physical assets
- people

On 32 intermittent dates during the first phase before assuming the second headship, he noted a total of 512 items ranging across the five categories. These were gathered from visits to the school in advance, meetings about the school held elsewhere and from private work at home — for example, on school documents. During the second phase (ie his first half-term as Head) he recorded further items relating to his five management categories on 32 consecutive days; this balanced the number of intermittent days in the first phase. In the second phase a total of 653 items were noted. The results are shown in Figure 1.1. Each section consists of a group of eight dates.

The number of times noted on any one day varied from one to 75, the first phase showing greater variation than the second. Experience in the first phase was erratic since opportunities had to be snatched to prepare for the second headship while he was still fully engaged in running the school he was about to leave. As would be expected, by far the largest number of items identified arose from the actual visits to the school. These visits would have been less profitable without the particular device he used as part of his preparation for the second headship. Figure 1.1. indicates how well the Head is along the way to having a complete overview and understanding of the new school by systematically noting matters needing attention.[1]

Management model for the primary school

Management of the primary school is something of a seamless garment. Every single matter, however large or small, simple or complex, relates to many other matters. Any one of them may turn out to have greater significance than was at first thought, when taken in conjunction with other matters.

FIGURE 1.1 One Head's working model of his management task

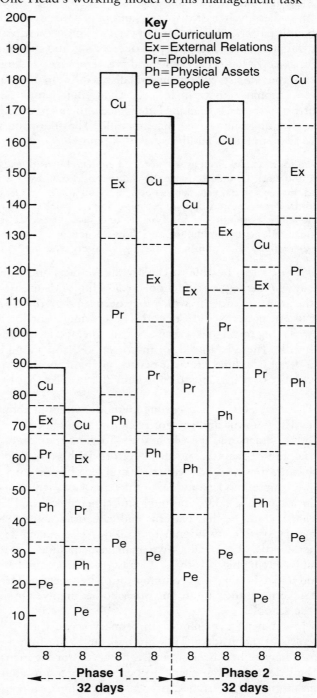

Although daily life for the Head of a primary school seems to consist of an endless welter of disparate and unrelated events, there are clearly definable patterns. Discovering or even inventing these patterns and creating classifications for the myriad of facts — and subsequently changing them as new facts, new events and greater understanding demand — is part of the interest, excitement and discipline of management. It becomes a professional activity in its own right. But it may be in such sharp contrast to the class teaching experience of many newly appointed Heads that the job seems to be incompatible. The following statement by a newly appointed Head illustrates this point:

I used to lie awake at night — not with anxiety, but with excitement — planning the work I would do with the children next day. Even when I was deputy head this used to happen. When I became Head all this suddenly changed. I had no difficulty in going to sleep at night — in fact, I was very glad to. The trouble came in the mornings. I found I had to drag myself to school on many a day. I just couldn't get the feeling for the job as a whole and give myself to it with the same creativity and enthusiasm that I gave to my teaching.

It is essential to be able to classify all the facts and to be able to think about whole categories of school life. Dealing with undifferentiated details in the arbitrary order in which they occur in the primary school, without the use of patterns and categories, is too much for the human mind to bear. Trying to do so is a recipe for muddle, ineffectiveness and probable ill-health. There is a need to find or impose some kind of order on the fine detail of school life as it occurs, giving it meaning and creating the possibility of being able to cope with all the tasks that have to be undertaken.

There are no right and wrong methods for going about this classification. The patterns and categories chosen should be those which help the Head to understand the whole school organisation and to see it steadily. Earlier in this chapter, one Head's efforts in this direction were described. The categories he used were crude and few, but they nevertheless helped him to gain an understanding of the school as a whole and provided him with a basis for taking rational and coherent action. The one proviso, perhaps, could be that patterns and categories chosen should not be so arbitrary or unconventional that no-one else can understand them. In other words, the Head's own management model really needs to be readily intelligible to others. Ideally, it can become the instrument of good understanding and communication between the Head and the staff, the governors, the parents and other bodies involved in the life and work of the school.

Most management models in primary schools are dominated by the interests of the insiders. They are built up by staff on the inside looking out. It may be beneficial in future, however, for the management models to be oriented to the client, to be even more conscious of the market than in the past. Current attitudes, expectations, values and practices in the community at large can best be summed up in the word 'consumerism'. If this is recognised as the force which will prevail in society and affect schools, it would seem logical for the Head to let it influence the approach he or she makes to developing an overview and understanding of the school as a whole.

Those who are outside looking in ask homely — but nonetheless critical — questions. It is suggested that the following list of ten such questions cover between them the entire life and work of the primary school. With these in mind, a management model can be built for internal use by the Head in a personal capacity as general manager and more widely by the staff as a whole. Figure 1.2 shows such a a management model, drawn up in answer to the following questions:

1 What does the school have?
2 What are the people like?
3 What do they believe in?
4 What do they teach?
5 How do they look after the children?
6 What is the organisation like?
7 Do they have things sorted out?
8 How well are they doing?
9 How do they get on with everyone else?
10 How is it all made to work?

FIGURE 1.2 Management model for the primary school

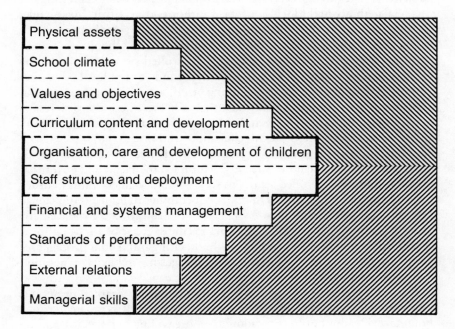

Physical assets

School climate

Values and objectives

Curriculum content and development

Organisation, care and development of children

Staff structure and deployment

Financial and systems management

Standards of performance

External relations

Managerial skills

Physical assets

The physical assets of the primary school consist of its buildings, facilities, furniture, equipment and materials. At first, most people think of the school as a building or suite of buildings. It may or may not have playing fields, hardcourt areas, car parking and other facilities attached. The building may be architecturally undistinguished and lacking in eye appeal, buried amid hundreds of other smaller and larger buildings in an inner-city location. The school may even be difficult to see, being surrounded by a high wall which physically limits the horizons of children and staff from within. The wall may guarantee their safety but do nothing to blot out the constant roar of the traffic. In contrast, the school may be of recent design and construction, pleasing to the eye and enhanced by a pleasant location in the green surroundings of a rural or semi-rural area with plenty of fresh air and attractive views to lift the spirit.

All who are in any way connected with the school — from new staff, parents, new children and governors to visiting advisers and members of Her Majesty's Inspectorate — form their initial impressions of it as they approach the building for the first time. If the school's reputation (for good or ill) has gone before it, these first impressions of the building and its site and location will be allowed to reinforce or modify that reputation in the mind of the visitor. Such feelings as delight, sympathy, envy or regret are variously roused — much depending upon the particular interest which the visitor has in the school. For example, the parent may deplore the appalling state of the fabric and condition of the external paintwork. The adviser certainly will also deplore it, while regretting the financial inability of the local education authority to rectify it. Meanwhile, the new child may take pleasure in spotting the play equipment which forms part of the permanent outdoor fixtures of the school.

In the case of county and voluntary controlled primary schools, the Head is almost certain to be wholly in the hands of the local education authority with regard to the building itself, its maintenance, general appearance and condition, and facilities. Yet even here the differences between Heads begin to be seen. With limited funds available for repairs and external decoration, local education authorities have to choose between schools on one basis or another. The chances of obtaining building replacement are remote. Such a situation led the Head and governors of one voluntary controlled school to seek voluntary aided status in order to get a new building. Limited though opportunities to improve or acquire new physical assets may be it is open to the Head to make the case for priority for his or her school. This demands the exercise of all the political arts, in concert with the governors — cultivating influential people, preparing persuasive and impressive documents, getting publicity, generating indirect pressures, and asserting personal appeals.

A good manager is one who never takes things for granted or accepts any boundary as given. He or she can judge when it is safe to cross a boundary. Heads of primary schools are more willing to take the initiative and fight the case with the local education authority than they used to be. Sometimes they are driven to this by sheer desperation. There is, however, a more general adaptation to current circumstances by many Heads; they are more active and outgoing on behalf of their schools in contrast to the more taciturn and benign conduct of their predecessors in the 1960s and 1970s. Even so, some primary school Heads are still passive over these matters. They seem intimidated by the local education authority to the point of insecurity and inaction.

The effective Head is one prepared to do battle to increase the physical assets of the school and to improve their quality

School climate

The buildings and all other physical properties of the school recede into the background as soon as the members of the school — its staff and children — are brought into the picture. The human spirit can rise above poor physical surroundings as many primary schools prove. When the physical surroundings are all that could be desired it does not automatically follow that a good spirit will pervade the school.

The human feeling in the school is an important matter. It is often called the ethos of the school because it is rooted in values, but meteorological imagery is commonly used so the term school climate is appropriate. In short, it is the spirit of the school and can be independent of surroundings and conditions. Every teacher, child, parent or non-teaching member of staff knows what it feels like to be there. People speak of the children as being 'warm and friendly' or 'unsettled this term'. Similarly, teachers may have a 'stormy' staff meeting or a meeting with parents in which there is a 'nice atmosphere'. A school may be described as 'happy' or as having 'no heart'.

Efforts have been made to classify the various school climates which may be found in practice. Some schools seem to be dominated by fear and secrecy, others by rigid conformity, some by unrestrained and arbitrary behaviour, yet others by good fellowship and trust — and so on.

Undoubtedly, some aspects of the environment may have a contributory — if not a causal—effect. Overcrowding may become a very powerful factor influencing the school climate. In recent times, industrial action by teaching staff has become an important factor. These are examples of circumstances which may affect the school climate if nothing else prevails. The spirit of the school, however, need not be wholly subject to the ebb and flow of environmental factors. The Head in the primary school is uniquely able to master-mind the school climate. It is the mark of effectiveness in the Head that an identifiable and pervasive school climate is established and that the kind of school climate generated is conducive to the realisation of the educational objectives of the school.

The effective Head is one who is able to establish a marked and pervasive climate in the school consistent with the school's educational objectives

Values and objectives

The school climate rests on values which are either collectively held or held by the majority of the staff. It is unlikely that the school climate rests on the values of the Head alone or any other minority group, except in the sense that where minority values are powerfully asserted the resulting tension and indeterminateness of the climate may itself become the prevailing school climate.

A value is a view of the desirable. Every person in the school — teachers, children, governors, parents — holds values about themselves: themselves in relation to others, their futures and the conduct of affairs in both the immediate and the wider environments. A value held should logically lead to a value pursued. Some kind of objective is formulated which gives expression to values and can be achieved by the appropriate and necessary action of oneself and/or others. If people have values but take no action in relation to them they are said to lack character. If they have values but clearly take inappropriate or unnecessary action they are charged with being irrational.

Values are at the heart of organisation and management in the primary school. All discussion and debate, argument, contention, concern and schism are to do with the need to clarify, select and prioritise values. They are enshrined in the aims and objectives of the school and often come to be known as the philosophy of the school. The articulated and dominant values in the school are critical from two points of view. From the point of view of the client or consumer — the parent and the child and those who represent them and their interests — they are critical because they are presumed to govern the outcomes for the children. These outcomes include what the children will learn, how they will learn, the kinds of behaviour they will be encouraged and discouraged to display and what sort of outlook on life they will be influenced to have. They are also critical from the staff's point of view, since values govern the quality and number of objectives which will be pursued by the school.

Objectives give direction and are associated with purpose and commitment. They are measures by which the organisation knows whether it has succeeded or not. There should be a match in the school between its declared philosophy or set of values and what actually happens. The way the school operates in all aspects should look as if it is meant to achieve the objectives set. Visible and readily available information such as a calendar of events or a timetable, as well as what can be immediately seen, ought to bear out the values of the school because its declared objectives are clearly in evidence.

New parents and staff are usually keen to discover the dominant values of the school, to find out whose they are and how they acquire their status. After seeing the buildings and getting the feel of the school climate, there is a natural curiosity to account for what is seen. The power-house of values which may or may not be present lies in the hearts and minds of the Head and staff.

Under present legislation, every school is expected to have expressed its values in clear objectives. These are expected to be available in written form and kept up to date by a proper process within the school. Values manifest in objectives are the key to the primary school. Nothing the Head can do or say makes a more important contribution to his or her effectiveness than originating or orchestrating the values and objectives of the school. They need to be a reality and reiterated often.

The effective Head is one whose school has firm values and clear objectives which are reiterated often

Curriculum content and development

The curriculum is the natural centre of attention in the primary school. It culminates in the productive work of the school and justifies its existence. The three important aspects of it are its actual content, how it is taught and managed and how it develops.

It used to be the case that when the technicalities of the curriculum were raised the layman was left behind and the professional took over. Today, parents, their representatives, the governors, pressure groups and other bodies in the community are increasingly willing and able to comment constructively and sometimes destructively on the curriculum — its content, relevance, ambiguity, duplication and relative usefulness for the education and future interests of their children. Furthermore, the method by which the curriculum is taught used to be beyond the interference of the layman but even this is no longer beyond comment, criticism and organised objection, as the following extract from one Head's experience illustrates.

The Head of a small rural school received a telephone call from the chairperson of the school governors. She complained that a parent had contacted her to say that her child had been out in the fields for the day instead of working in the classroom.
The Head protested that the child's class had been engaged under proper supervision in investigative studies in the natural environment. It was a tried and tested method of teaching and learning in primary education.
'That's not what the parent thinks' came the rejoinder, 'and it's not what I think either, so I am calling for your immediate suspension as head of school until an enquiry has been held.'

Because of the Education Act 1986, school governors with substantial parental representation, will in future have increased statutory duties with regard to the curriculum, presenting the Head with either a source of interference or a new power base. The effectiveness of the Head will be seen in his or her ability to secure the constant effort of the staff to attune curriculum content to developments in knowledge, the contemporary interests of children and the demands of modern society. His or her judgement will still be needed amid the numerous and often conflicting expectations of the curriculum.

The effective Head is one who secures agreement with staff and governors on the curriculum and its continual development

Organisation, care and development of children

This is closely related to school climate and the curriculum. The justifiable view to take over the organisation, care and development of the children is the longest possible one i.e. the entire time that the child will be a member of the school. During that time, all the resources of the school are potentially available for each child. What each child's share of those resources actually turns out to be is a matter of good organisation. The mix and quality of the ingredients must be that which will contribute best to the social, intellectual, emotional and physical growth of the child. The school's policy on grouping children for all the variety of teaching and learning purposes is crucial in this respect, together with the range of staff and opportunities offered.

Formal care structures may be established beyond the normal practice of assigning first-line pastoral care to the class teacher, for example year groups or the separation of infants and juniors. Whatever these structures may be there will also be a need for special mechanisms for exceptional cases — the child in need of selective support, close supervision or remedial tuition, and provision for gifted children.

The differential treatment of all children is the focus of concern. It may be that the Head and other members of staff are in possession of interpersonal skills which they seek to cultivate in the children. These would include being able and willing to listen and to understand viewpoints other than their own, to offer praise and encouragement as well as sympathy and rebuke when necessary. There would be opportunity for children to undertake duties on behalf of others, to be responsible for something and to exercise self-discipline.

The objective is always to establish and maintain a safe and supportive but challenging environment. It needs to be flexible enough to vary the quantity and quality of options so as to cater for the diverse range of children. A monitoring system needs to be installed so that remedial or corrective measures may be taken with speed and sensitivity in response to a child's behaviour and educational performance as necessary.

The effective Head is one who gives the child access to the best available resources, monitors their use and takes corrective action

Staff structure and deployment

The staff structure is the way the school distributes jobs, authority and positions among the men and women who make up the teaching and non-teaching workforce. At present, most salary matters such as pay scale rates, increments and increases lie far beyond the control of the individual school. Much of the staff structure, therefore, is determined from outside the school. Nevertheless, a considerable area of discretion remains with the Head and there is plenty of scope for job rotation within the school. In the main, the actual deployment of the teaching staff is in the hands of the Head, though this is generally not so in the case of non-teaching staff.

By the adroit deployment and use of staff, the Head hopes to realise the objectives of the school. This is a key operation, calling for good judgement and a knowledge of the strengths and weaknesses of staff members and the needs of the children.

The formal staff structure can be made readily available, often in diagrammatic form, as one of the descriptors of the school. This is a selective picture of how teachers are intended to relate to one another when at work, the particular part of the total work of the school which each should have, and, by implication, the level and kind of expertise which they need to do their work. In practice, however, the structure will be very different, modified by the actual personalities of real people coping variously with the endless flow of demands which strain and stress them and test their mettle. The overriding consideration in structuring and deploying the staff is to enable every person to be as effective as possible. Finding each one the job he or she can do well is one alternative. The other is to supply further training or resources so that he or she can do the job already being undertaken better. Performance may or may not be currently monitored and appraised. Preparations for, or the actual practice of, a formal staff appraisal scheme may or may not already be occurring. Underachievement may be ignored or acted upon. There may or may not be plans for staff development in anticipation of changing school needs or in support of innovations. Staff absence, lateness and turnover rates are important indicators of the quality of the staff structure and deployment. Adjusting the structure is the Head's key task in the work of staff management.

The effective Head is one who liberates and maximises the motivation and abilities of staff through the structure and deployment decisions adopted.

Financial and systems management

Two important features in the task of management in the primary school are finances and systems. Money is necessary for running the school. If managed properly, money fulfils the efforts of many, but if managed badly it impairs them. Good financial management is an essential ingredient of effectiveness. Procedures for the management of finance are generally laid down by the local education authority. Judgement on what to spend the money on and when to spend it lies largely within the school. Systems management refers to the need to think about conventions, routines, rituals and procedures as a whole in the school — in other words, any pre-determined ways of doing something. These procedures include the handling of money, stock and equipment but also range extensively over the behavioural aspects of school life.

No school can be run on the basis of deciding afresh each morning what shall take place, when it is to be done and how it shall be done for that day. Indeed, many events are already well set by wider social convention and deeply ingrained habit, such as the times for starting and ending the school day. Where adopted, experimental times along the lines of the continental school day soon become the new norm. Life would be unbearable and unworkable in the primary school if nothing could be reduced to habit and routine. Conventions, routines and procedures are important tools of management. They help to get large numbers of children working in an orderly and predictable way so that results can be achieved.

In a primary school systems are manifest in a multitude of ways, great and small, trivial and important. They pervade staff handbooks and the school brochure, as well as other information to parents. The systems form part of the induction process for every teacher and child. The new child, like the new member of staff, if joining the school in the middle of the year, feels dislocated for such time as it takes to learn the conventions, routines and procedures. These conventions can range from the notification of absence, the ordering and storage of stock and the handling of accidents to which side along a corridor the children must walk, where physical education shoes and clothing are to be kept and how children should treat visitors to the school.

The volume of conventions, routines and procedures adopted — like the spending of money — is a matter of judgement. If there are too few, continual turbulence can abound in the school. If there are too many, initiative and creativity may be damaged, to the detriment of the school. Then all energies are driven into the maintenance of the system which is meant to be servant rather than master. If they are too pettifogging and exacting, irritation and deliberate avoidance will occur. Systems need to be valued (employed sparingly but sufficiently to get efficiency in the use of time and energy), kept in their place, and revised and adjusted from time to time.

The effective Head is one who has a complete grasp of the school's finances and systems, has up-to-date knowledge of them and makes them active instruments of school policy

Standards of performance

Every member of staff and every child is expected to make a contribution to the work of the school. This contribution cannot be determined by the arbitrary choice of the individual concerned. It needs to conform to standards which in turn are derived from the objectives which the school sets for itself. The individual's actual work output in one way or another is subject to inspection and review. Standards of performance may be concerned with either the quantity of work or the quality of work or both. Standards can apply to conduct as well as work.

Standards of performance can be determined subjectively by the person or persons who are in a legal and practical position to do so — the Head in relation to staff and children and the teaching staff in relation to the children they teach. In contrast, they can be determined objectively by setting measurable targets in advance of each specific task being undertaken by agreement with the teacher or child undertaking it. In many cases it is possible to set positive standards. In these cases what is wanted is known so that a clear target of achievement for the teacher and child can be agreed. In other cases negative standards apply when all that is known is what is not wanted. This gives a maximum area of discretion for the person concerned — unlike the imposition of positive standards. It is also possible to have so-called 'zero' standards — setting out what must not happen at all — which convey what is forbidden and impose a minimum area of total constraint on the teacher or child.

This aspect of management in the primary school, if undertaken in any thorough and systematic way for such a large number of individual staff and children, is bound to involve a degree of record keeping. Every school depends to a certain extent upon documentation. Teachers generally are more preoccupied with class contact responsibilities than with paperwork in support of their teaching. This is in part due to the existing notion of the working day. It is especially of concern to the teaching Head who must find time beyond the teaching contact day to look after the paperwork for the school as a whole.

Data management is an important part of headship. It is vital that the school maintains accurate and up-to-date information on all aspects of its work. The school's data system should include pupil records, staff records, records of meetings, school publicity and information material, staff management material, communications to children and parents, the local authority and other external organisations, curriculum development material and documents to do with the governing body. In short the system would consist of sufficient documentation, duly collected, stored and updated, to provide an entire management information facility for the school.

Assessment is a wide-ranging activity in the primary school: from the teacher's word of approval or disapproval of a child's action or performance in his or her work, to full-scale testing and grading by formal methods. The monitoring and measurement of work is characteristic of all organisations. The methods employed depend upon the purpose to be served and the nature of the work involved. They can be crude and subjective or sophisticated and objective; they may consist of words or figures. The introduction of the pupil profile or record of achievement, together with greater emphasis on staff appraisal or review, will increase the amount of documentation needed in the primary school.

Surmounting all these forms of assessment is the most inclusive exercise which can take place — the evaluation of the school as a whole. What is our school like? How are we doing? How do we know how well we are doing? are questions which the Head and staff are bound to ask themselves sooner or later, and to which the public, through the local education authority, will want to know the answers.

Records, assessment and evaluation are all aspects of effective performance at one level or another. Performance is the most critical concern of management. Consequently, the documentation that goes with it needs to be subject to care and attention.

The effective Head is one who keeps standards of performance by staff and children in the forefront of his or her thinking, based upon adequate information, and takes regular action to correct underperformance and to praise good performance

External relations

It is something of a revolution in thinking and practice that a primary school should be *explicitly* sensitive to and guided by forces outside the school. There was a time when what went on inside the school was a mystery best left to the Head and the teaching staff. The Head could actually take it upon himself or herself to prevent entry into the school. Parents were particularly subject to exclusion. The vestiges of this practice still remain in a few primary schools — for example, the not-yet-removed yellow line around the perimeter of the school playground which parents were forbidden to cross.

Good schools have always taken note of parents and have been receptive to their inquiries, interests and visits. They have sought warm relationships with other schools, the local education authority, the police, the press and local shopkeepers.

The network of actual or potential external contacts, bodies and agencies of all kinds connected with the school's interests has multiplied out of all recognition; for some, they may even be the lifeblood of the school. Most schools in the primary sector have the opportunity to cull a computer from a generous donor, or to obtain waste materials from local industry which the children can use in school. Financially, it is not uncommon in some parts of the country for schools to multiply their official capitation grants several times over through private funding operations, especially with the help of parent organisations.

The enlargement of governing body memberships, and their official duties in relation to the school, means that in future the Head, in all probability, will be involved more than ever before in external activities. The objective will be to build up relations in the interests of the school. This dimension of headship will certainly be more political than ever before, calling for the Head's skills in speaking, persuading, chairing meetings, assessing the strength of coalitions and demonstrating shrewd judgement. These have to be added to those attributes already in demand —professional knowledge, integrity, and patent dedication to the education of children. To fulfil this dimension of headship takes time. It should not be undertaken at the expense of the internal management of the school: it may, however, lead to a redistribution of duties between the Head and the deputy.

The effective Head is one who builds a complete network of external contacts to serve the interests of the school

Managerial skills

Managerial skills are needed to bind together the organisation (which consists of many different people), so that its desired objectives can be reached. These skills take the form of human abilities and behaviour, exercised in one degree or another by everyone at his or her own level of responsibility. They are applicable in all parts of the life and work of the primary school. Some of them — such as being persuasive — are already likely to be practised by the good classroom teacher in the course of daily teaching. Many others, however, are not — for example, being able to conduct a work performance interview with a member of staff.

The management of the school needs to be a form of corporate responsibility. This involves identifying and using managerial skills among the staff as fully as possible. It may be possible to build these up in such a way that a strong team spirit develops. This, in turn, requires a particular set of managerial skills of the Head. If there is a formally established management team, consisting only of the Head and deputy head or involving others as well, there should be a distribution of duties which is known and recognised in practice throughout the school. Short and long term planning should be in evidence, involving the need for knowledge of developments within the school, the wider community and the educational world. The ability to approach problems constructively, to make decisions and to implement them effectively should be in evidence.

Skills in listening, leading discussions, chairing meetings, writing documents and addressing larger gatherings should be developed. A corporate ability to gather, analyse and interpret the views of children, staff, parents and others in the community is required, together with a regular pattern of meetings, other means of collecting information, processing problems, and the making and implementing of decisions.

The effective Head is one who takes pride in and develops his or her own managerial skills, values the managerial skills of others and establishes the means to develop them.

Basis of effective management

A model has been offered of the complete range of areas which need to be comprehended for a whole view of the primary school: it constitutes the content of the management task of the Head. The managerial performance of the Head can only be judged for its effectiveness if all ten areas are taken into account. It takes time for a Head to tackle all the areas. Some will be in more need of urgent attention than others. Heads will vary in their level of competence and achievement in the different areas. Nevertheless, it is with reference to the entire range of management areas that most Heads would wish to review their own managerial performance. In seeking to build up his or her own effectiveness, a Head might use the following checklist, based on the model in this chapter.

1   Have I increased the physical assets of the school and/or improved their quality?
2   Have I constructed a marked and appropriate climate in keeping with the school's objectives?
3   Have I achieved the recognition and adoption of firm values and clear realistic objectives and do I reiterate these at every suitable opportunity?
4   Have I secured agreement among the staff and between the staff and the governors on curriculum content and method, and are these in the process of continual review and improvement?
5   Have I devised a policy for distributing the teaching and physical resources of the school fairly among all the children in the course of their time in the school, and made it work in practice?
6   Have I structured and deployed the staff in a way that enables them to give of their best?

7   Have I mastered the finances of the school and made them an active means of development? Have I brought the conventions, routines, rituals and procedures of the school under periodic review and modified them as necessary to obtain the smooth running of the school overall?

8   Are standards of performance with respect to staff and children a matter of constant consideration? Is performance monitored, under-performance acted upon and good performance recognised?

9   Have I built up a complete network of external contacts who can serve the school and help to give it a good public image?

10   Have I developed my own managerial skills and brought out those of the staff through a staff development policy and job opportunities?

2
Considering the key concepts

Headship is all about action. Every working day in the primary school is a buzz of activity. Children in classrooms and home-base areas, encouraged by the teaching staff, are urged into action. Headship is very much a matter of enabling, leading and facilitating all this activity, which makes up the life of the school. Because it is purposeful, this activity is preceded by preparation. Action follows careful thought. This gives the work of the school direction, coherence and rationality.

The task of management requires the kind of thinking prior to a specific action which will enable everyone who is to be involved with that action to make sense of it. The Head as general manager needs to be able to think managerially in addition to — if not in place of — being able to think pedagogically. He or she is dependent on having some knowledge of a few essential concepts, which, when understood and made part of the habitual intellectual process, can form the basis for professional, managerial discipline. The distinctive accomplishment and justification of such discipline is being able to carry purpose into effective action.

Three concepts are presented in this chapter. If they are thoroughly understood and continually applied to all the work of running the school, the Head can have the advantage of knowing what to think about at all times, knowing what he or she is doing, and knowing how to make a consistent impact. The three concepts are resources, objectives and results.

The concept of resources

For management purposes, the word resources means all that is needed and used to run the school. This goes beyond the meaning of the word for teaching purposes which already has common currency in the primary school. In the teaching context it is given special but limited meaning to refer to consumable materials such as paper or paint, non-consumable materials such as books or rulers, and perhaps light, portable equipment such as tape recorders or slide projectors — in short, everything used by, with and for the children in their work. These resources are located either centrally on an access and retrieval basis or departmentally on a year group, team or unit basis for continuous use. They may be best called teaching/learning resources and thus distinguished from the use of the word as an inclusive managerial concept covering all that is needed and used to establish and develop the school in its entirety.

As a managerial concept, resources includes two kinds — the human and the physical. Some organisations have only a small human element in the total resources needed for their work and output, relying chiefly on physical resources: others have a balance between human and physical resources. Primary schools are among the latter. The staff and children, together with other people involved with the school, combine to make the primary school predominantly human-resource oriented. Yet the physical resources cannot be disregarded. The cost of the school's buildings alone could typically be a million pounds, to say nothing of the ongoing maintenance and other costs of the physical assets of the school. Altogether, the total resources of the school are very substantial. The proper use and development of them are important duties of the Head, as previously indicated in Chapter 1.

Resources in concept refers to everything which is actually or potentially available for the task in hand. In its limited use for pedagogical purposes, teachers in the primary school are familiar with it; in its extended use for school management purposes they are less so. Teachers are less habituated to the inclusive thinking that is needed. This may be because such a mode of thinking makes them feel ill-at-ease, as if they were carried out of the realms of primary education. Life seems to have an inhuman ring to it when people are thought of as resources. In truth, the use of the word resources is purely technical. As such it becomes a jargon word but jargon exists in every walk of life to make it easier for practitioners working in the same field to talk to one another and to understand one another as efficiently and as completely as possible.

There is no imputation whatsoever, in the concept of resources, that people do not matter and that finance and inanimate objects do. One of the highest expectations in management is that people will be treated as the foremost resource, with straight dealing, justice and love — as befits the primary school. People normally want to give of their best. It is management's job to enable them to do so. Anything less than the accomplishment of this is bad management.

The elements of resources

In essence, resources in the primary school can be said to have four elements — human energy, objects, finance and time. These are common to all organisations but subject to vastly varying mixtures and differing expressions. Among primary schools, how each is expressed and the mixture adopted is common enough to give them a distinctive character of their own, yet even between primary schools substantial variation exists within the general pattern. Figure 2.1 shows the particular form the four elements can take in the primary school. In Figure 2.1 only a dotted line separates the four pure elements in the centre to show that they are all of a piece; in practice they interact in infinite combinations. The four wings provide the main descriptors or categories for the elements as they exist in primary schools.

FIGURE 2.1   Classification of resources in the primary school

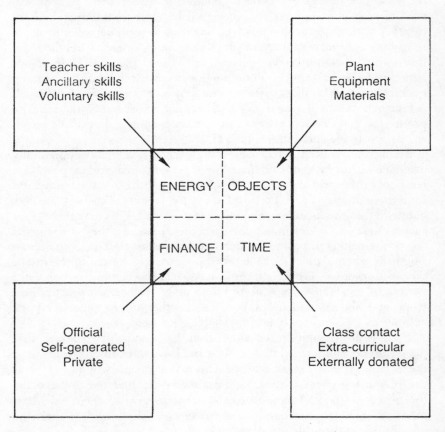

Energy is expressed in three classes of human skills — those of the teaching staff; those of the ancillary staff, including secretary, caretaker, cleaning staff, welfare assistants and school meals staff, together with visiting personnel such as medical, legal and social services staff; and those of volunteers such as parents or anyone from the community who offers services in any way and for any purpose. Human energy is the most unpredictable, imprecise but important resource.

Human energy can be expressed in three different kinds of skill — or at least skill applied in three different ways. First, there are specific skills. These are unique skills in the sense that either no-one else within the school is competent to exercise them or, if someone is competent to exercise them, he or she cannot do so on account of being fully committed to something else. For a teacher, this would mean having the knowledge and ability to coordinate, say, mathematics as opposed to physical education, or teach second year infants as opposed to fourth year juniors. The same applies to ancillary staff and voluntary contributions to the school.

The school should guard and promote its stock of specific skills. Everyone should have and should contribute to them in sufficient depth. If everyone can do everything this can mean great administrative convenience, but it may imply that specific skills are shallow. In addition, the usual motivation which an individual derives from being able to make a particular contribution may be absent.

Second, there are generic skills. These are the skills which can legitimately be expected of everyone. For example, every teacher is expected to be able to handle a class. Indeed, every adult who enters the school for purposes of work is expected to be able to relate to children and to treat them with respect. Generic skills are multiple, involving business responsibility, staff discussions, negotiations, meetings, relating to parents and extra-curricular activity.

Third, there are social skills, in the narrow sense of the term. All the adults who work in the school or who visit it must relate to one another on a suitable basis which reflects the objectives of the school and contributes to the kind of climate which is desired. Everyone needs to help in the promotion of unity within the school, to make working life within it as pleasant as possible, to heal the inevitable differences of opinion and even breaches caused in the course of developing the work of the school and to generate a friendly and purposeful climate.

Other than energy which is expressed as human skills, the remaining elements are objects, finance and time. Objects are all the physical aspects of the school. The plant consists of the buildings, facilities, internal spaces, and power supplies for lighting, heating and cooking. Equipment includes general items such as furniture, computers, overhead projectors, televisions, the minibus, photocopiers and the like, together with subject-specific items such as the kiln, drama-blocks and properties, and physical education, science and mathematics apparatus. Materials includes everything which is consumed, from paper and paint for the classroom use of the children to foodstuffs needed for the preparation of their meals.

Finance consists of official sources — notably for salaries, building costs, repairs and maintenance, and the capitation allowance; self-generated sources, such as jumble sales, the sale of goods made in the school and, maybe, lettings; and private sources, such as gifts, initiatives from parents, bequests and the considerable sums which teachers themselves directly and indirectly spend on their teaching and other school commitments.

Finally, time can be said to consist of class contact or the formal school day; extra-curricular activities such as concerts, collecting items for school, clubs and sports fixtures, school journeys and visits, and marking and preparing lessons; and externally donated time of those not on the payroll who are willing to spend time in the interests of the school in one capacity or another — for example helping out with curriculum activities during or after school or undertaking manual jobs such as decorating the school and putting up shelving. Many teachers also contribute externally donated time for the latter purposes.

Resources in use

Altogether, energy, objects, finance and time form the total resources which can be put to work. The particular mix of them distinguishes one primary school from the next and the managerial capacity of one Head from another. The indissoluble links between them can provide the basis for endless managerial ingenuity and invention and all four need to be kept in mind as a matter of regular intellectual habit. The kind of links which can be made between them can be illustrated simply. For example, human energy is the main resource in the primary school. Very often there are deficiencies in the objects — the school building may be inadequate or in a state of decay; there may be a shortage of equipment or materials — yet human energy can overcome these deficiencies and guarantee that schooling continues. The best plant, equipment and materials available, even in plenteous quantity, do not of themselves ensure that good schooling will take place. The question always remains, however, as to how much better the schooling can be when they *are* increased in quantity or improved in quality. When this occurs the human energy factor is maintained, rather than diminished.

Finance may be used to secure more human energy or more physical objects but the same sum of money cannot buy both at once. Freedom to exercise financial discretion in primary schools is increasing in some parts of the country and may do so more widely in due course. A cost–benefit analysis should accompany every expenditure. Too much of one kind of resource can inhibit the contribution which other resources can make. It is the overall effect of an increase or a reduction of a resource which needs to be borne in mind. One Head bought so many audio tapes that there were insufficient opportunities (time) for teachers and children to use them all.

In reciprocal fashion, some of the stock of human energy in the school can be used in many schools — but by no means all — to raise more finance, which can then buy more human energy and materials. Diverting some energy from teaching itself might be justified. Similarly, physical objects can be disposed of to raise more finance, particularly objects which are surplus to requirements or are underused.

Time is the one ubiquitous resource which, unlike human energy and

physical objects, does not wear out and, unlike finance, cannot be accumulated. Yet time is money. Time is also human energy in a manner of
speaking. It also governs the decay of physical objects. The unnecessary
staff meeting, the excessive stock of unused exercise books, the underused,
expensive machine or equipment with built-in obsolescence, and the cash
in the current account which could be invested — all illustrate the importance of time as a resource and its interconnection with the other kinds
of resources.

Creating the best mix of resources to get the best overall results is the
skilled work of the Head. Resources are always finite, even though trying
to increase them is a part of the general manager's task. Working within
finite possibilites is the routine discipline required. Nevertheless, it is
worth regarding resources as flexible, even though some resources appear
to be fixed in quantity — for example, the school building, the capitation
allowance and salaries for staff. Yet many schools have found ways to
supplement even fixed resources — for example, acquiring the use of
premises elsewhere for field studies, raising funds by local initiative and
inviting the help of voluntary workers in the school.

An important aspect of the quantity of resources is the question of
waste. By cutting down waste, one is in effect increasing the quantity of
resources. A prerequisite for doing this is training staff and children to
be cost conscious, whether over the use of paper, electricity, the telephone
or anything else. But notably, of all resources, time itself should not be
wasted. The adroit use of time, careful timing, punctuality and the best
use of time can all be watchwords or catchphrases foremost in the mind
of everyone. Staff might give even more time than they already give to
their jobs and thereby increase the resources for the school. Equally, they
might be encouraged to accomplish more in the time which they already
give. The improved use of time (without becoming neurotic about it) is
always desirable.

Resources sometimes seem to be more limited than they really are,
simply because it is not always apparent what resources are at the school's
disposal. The problem is one of ignorance and accessibility. For example,
there may be teachers who acquire new knowledge and skills through
in-service education and training on a voluntary basis but whose staff
records are not brought up to date. A new Head may be appointed in
the meanwhile. If the teacher does not choose to mention his or her new
qualifications and interests, an additional resource may be lost. Or expensive pieces of equipment, such as the overhead projector, may be stored
on the shelf since their arrival — and still without a plug, as one Head
found on taking up appointment. Yet another newly appointed Head
found cupboards choked with materials purchased and hoarded by the
previous Head. Staff had no access to them other than through the Head,
whose parsimony in issuing them was a byword which discouraged experiment and enterprise.

A further way to increase resources, in effect, is to use them more fully.

In principle resources are scarce. No resource, therefore, should be idle or underused. Special facilities such as a fully equipped music room, wet area, mathematics room or playing field, or valuable equipment for teaching purposes such as a video or slide projector, ought to be as intensively used as possible — even constantly, subject only to avoiding the danger of premature damage through overuse and the neglect of maintenance.

Taking into account the range of disparate resources involved, it may be seen that ways and means can be found to vary and increase their volume. Above all, the mixing of resources is the crucial factor. The possibilities are always more numerous than they seem.

The very existence of a resource — a particular space, a staff skill, a piece of equipment or some material — can suggest its own use. The Head's task in relation to resources is demanding as well as creative. Certain aspects of this task have been identified in this chapter.

1   to increase the quantity and, or the quality of existing resources and to add new resources
2   to train staff and children to be cost conscious
3   to get the very best use out of every resource, subject only to the need to avoid their premature decay through overuse
4   to encourage the experimental mixing of resources together with the practice of cost–benefit analysis

Efficiency in using resources

The requirement that resources should be well managed is usually thought to stem from the need to save money. This in turn is linked to the need to create profits as far as commercial and manufacturing organisations are concerned. Schools are thought by many people to be exempt from such a concern. While it is true that schools are non-profit-making organisations, it is equally true that they, together with all other kinds of organisations, should display a responsible attitude towards the use of resources.

There is a moral side to the use of resources as well as the side which deals with the income–expenditure equation. It has two aspects. In the first place, a primary school's entire costs, for all practical purposes, are met by tax and ratepayers at large. The teaching staff are custodians of resources which might be used for alternative services sorely needing additional support. In the second place, the good management of resources makes life and work in the school more pleasant and bearable than it otherwise would be for all those involved. It adds to the quality of life. Foremost in this regard is the need to manage the human energy resource well, since this implies high motivation levels and resulting benefits for the children. At the present time, a number of substantial resource factors are prescribed and controlled from outside the school. Nevertheless, there remains great scope for the Head to exercise prudent resource management.

The concept of resources cannot be considered without mentioning the idea of efficiency. This can be a dreaded word, evoking, for many, thoughts of clipboards, scrutiny and interference, It is, in fact, a technical word and should be reserved for special use. It stands for the concern and process to see that a resource is fully and properly used. There is always a relationship between what goes into a job and what comes out of it. This is the efficiency ratio between input(s) and output(s). The idea is to get the best out of the inputs in terms of the outputs. Usually this means not looking at each resource in isolation but rather at how they are mixed. Resources seldom, if ever, act in isolation; hence the need for management. Primary schools are used to thinking and acting to raise output levels by looking for a more efficient, if more complex, mix of resources as inputs. Examples of this are individualised learning, self-help learning aids, exploratory teaching and learning methods and co-operative teaching — as opposed, say, to constant, one-mode didactic teaching and learning methods uniformly adopted throughout the school. Efficiency in the primary school is said to have improved when *either* it achieves more output, with resources (input) remaining unchanged *or* it achieves the same output with reduced resources (input).

Work output has two aspects — quantity and quality. Both need to be borne in mind in questions of efficiency. If the size of a class is increased and the quality standards of the educational output or achievement of the children are maintained without more teaching time or assistance or the addition of other resources, then an increase in efficiency can be said to have been achieved. The teacher's salary remains the same, the same time is used and the same classroom space is used. Yet in the final analysis it can never be true that something can be obtained for nothing. The teacher has to work harder over the same period of time.

On the other hand, instead of working *harder* it could be possible for the teacher to make *better* use of the time — working more selectively, more wisely, in effect cutting out waste of time and effort and using ideas, organisation and materials more productively. It is almost always better to encourage efficiency in the latter sense. The former may only imply more of the same — using existing ways and means but at a faster rate. This kind of efficiency may be self-defeating. Fatigue and disillusionment may set in, leading to the premature capitulation of the teacher and cessation of the newly found effort. The latter kind, *ie* improving quality, can produce longer-term and more durable results.

Efficiency is essentially about doing things right. It does not address itself to doing the right things. In other words, a primary school can be exceedingly efficient in producing the wrong results — the product that nobody wants. It is the kind of results that justify the school's existence, not the efficiency with which the results are achieved. The school's unit costs may be very low — calculated by comparing the overall costs of running the school with the number of children in it per year — but if the children know nothing, have no skills, are socially maladapted and have no qualifications or credentials for acceptance by another school, then there is neither point nor virtue in the school. Equally, they may have knowledge, skills, behaviour and credentials which are not judged to be suitable for their generation, age group, and the particular set of social, economic and political circumstances in which they find themselves.

Efficiency is only about the means, not the ends. It deals with objective matters. It is about measuring, counting and comparing. It is about cost, cost–benefit and accounting. It is only a part and not the sole preoccupation of the general manager, however. The main preoccupation is the school's effectiveness, which efficiency exists to serve, and this raises the whole question of objectives.

The concept of objectives

The word objectives enjoys strong currency in the primary school. It features in the lesson preparation of the teacher and in considerations of where the school should be going. It has usually been tied to aims, so that it has become customary to speak of the teacher's or the school's aims and objectives. Awareness has been heightened in recent years by the legal requirement laid on all local education authorities in the maintained sector to see that every school draws together and publishes a set of written aims. A large amount of time and energy has been spent in educational circles justifying the separation of aims from objectives and the need to have both. In curriculum theory they are seen to relate to one another. Aims embody intentions and stance. Objectives embody outcomes and results. The imagery of the archer's skill can be used to make the distinction. The important implication of having both and making them public is that comparisons can be made between what a school, in acknowledging what is needed, sets out to do and what it actually achieves. It is unfortunate if the aim is one thing and the objectives realised turn out to be quite another. It is embarrassing to miss the target.

The word aims, as in the phrase 'the aims of primary education', usually indicates the sometimes vague and very general aspirations, hopes and expectations of the clients of the education system or their representatives. These are directed towards the professional educators in the primary school. However few or numerous these may be, however sophisticated or naive in their expression and however weakly or forcibly expressed, they all really amount to the same thing. The school should provide an experience for each and every child which enhances the child's well-being every day he or she spends in school, enabling maximum growth and development to take place in each dimension of the complex human organism, and maximising the child's life-chances without diminishing those of other children.

In this case, objectives then become the vehicle by which such aims conveyed by the community are translated into something which is action-able — something which has meaning and can be cast in practical terms in a particular school. From the point of view of management discipline, this single concept of objectives is sufficient. If an objective envisaging the intended outcome or result is created in advance of the event, and indeed made public, nothing is lost. Much confusion may be saved. The clear articulation of what is being worked for implies what the intentions and the values are. In this case an objective may be thought of as a change of state brought about by the primary school at work.

An objective is a written or verbal statement specifying the change of state which will be brought about in either persons or objects by the deliberate and purposeful action of the primary school

Objectives as management tools

It is impossible to have an organisation without objectives. Organisations exist for a purpose and an objective expresses purpose. What does vary is the degree to which objectives are at the forefront of the manager's consciousness, the precision with which objectives are formed and how many there need to be.

These variations may be seen among primary schools today. In the past objectives have been implicit, but now they must be explicit; formerly they were unpublished, but now they must be published; they used to be informal, but now they are made formal.

In management universally, objectives are regarded as indispensable tools. They are used to marshal the human energies of the organisation and to give point, purpose and direction to everything which is done. To make objectives into usable and useful tools, a number of aspects should be considered. In the first place, it needs to be remembered that four different kinds of objectives govern the management of the primary school. These are the school's organisational mission objectives; its educational objectives for the children; its objectives for the use of resources; and the personal objectives of the adults and children within the school and of the adults outside who are concerned with it. These objectives may be related to one another as depicted in Figure 2.2.

First in importance are the school's *organisational mission objectives* which express the overall purposes of the school to the community outside the school and serve as constant guidelines for action within the school.

FIGURE 2.2   The different kinds of objectives at work in the primary
school

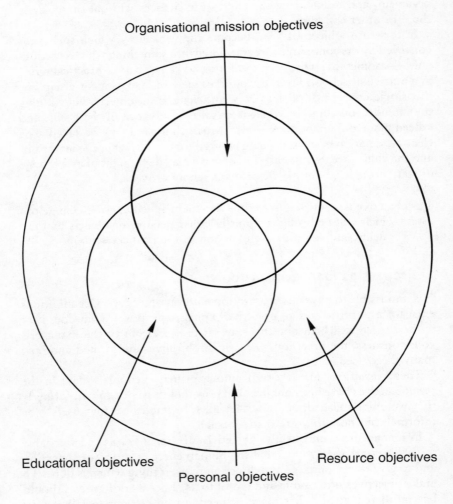

Examples of such objectives would be:
- to take part in community activities
- to serve and support community interests
- to train and encourage children to be law-abiding citizens
- to educate all children to a high standard of literacy and numeracy

It is worth bearing in mind the importance attached to their organisational
mission objectives by those outside education. A well known fast-food
chain has been successfully established around the world, due in part to
its founder's insistence on and constant reiteration of its four simple and
attainable organisational mission objectives of cleanliness, value for
money, quality of product and prompt service.

Next in importance are the objectives which specify what will have happened to the children by the time they complete their period of education in a particular school. The children will be different from what they were like when they entered that school. Some of these differences will be due to the work of the school and the children's experience of it. This outcome is essentially what the school exists for. These objectives are the school's *educational objectives* and strictly derive from the school's organisational mission objectives.

In third place are those objectives which derive in turn from the school's organisational mission objectives and its educational objectives. These are the *resource objectives*. The objectives govern the use made of finance, space, staff, facilities and every other resource. These objectives are vital because they are instrumental in achieving the educational objectives and so the school's organisational mission objectives. Resource objectives may range from getting a particular teacher to employ a different teaching method, or changing the function of a room, to restructuring the entire staff or reallocating the use of all the spaces in the school.

Affecting these three kinds of objectives are the fourth kind — the *personal objectives* of the individual persons involved. They may or may not be verbalised, but they nevertheless exist. Account must be taken of them in management. The Head, teacher, child, parent and every other person who works in the school or who is associated with it in any way has his or her own personal objectives which provide point, purpose and direction to work undertaken in the school, and affect relationships with others. Personal objectives surround and infuse the hierarchy of organisational mission, educational and resource objectives. There can never be complete agreement between personal objectives right across the board and the other three kinds of objectives, because there are so many points at which differences can arise. But as long as there is a pattern of general and substantial agreement, the school will enjoy harmony.

The existence of these four different kinds of objectives is potentially a source of considerable misunderstanding. Confusion can even reign between them. The Head plays a key part in distinguishing between the different kinds of objectives and relating them to one another. There is, however, the possibility of confusion and conflict in which the Head may be personally involved, as in the following example of a newly appointed Head.

1   *Personal objective*
    • to curb the reactionary influence of particular members of the teaching staff opposed to reform
2   *Educational objective*
    • to increase each child's investigative learning experience by 100%
3   *Resource objectives*
    • to modify the teaching approach from didactic to problem solving methods; to obtain and use new materials and equipment; to make use of available in-service staff training;

The teaching staff may choose to see the dominant objective at work as being the personal objective of the Head. It may be interpreted as based on a personal dislike of the teachers concerned, as resentment and jealousy over the amount of influence they have, or as rooted in the need of a new Head to make changes to justify his or her appointment. The teachers involved have their own personal objectives, which, variously, may not include any wish to change the way they teach. They may feel that the tried and trusted methods they have employed for many years have always stood them in good stead and have been right for the children. Their position may arise from complacency and indifference regarding educational outcomes, in which case there is obvious argument for compelling the change. In contrast, they may have a view of educational objectives which is rationally and properly linked to the methods they currently employ. In such a case, sincerity, commitment and professional integrity may well be at stake. This presents the Head with a substantial problem in the solution of which persuasion and evidence would have to play a leading part.

The Head is a central figure and the most influential source of advice, information and decision with respect to all four kinds of objectives in the primary school. It is he or she who is likely to originate and formulate the organisational mission objectives of the school, drawn up after due consideration has been given to the nature of the school, its problems, its catchment area and perceived opportunities, the Head's own philosophy, and the values and stance found in the governing body and staff. In doing this, the Head can demonstrate the characteristics of good leadership. This may include the powers of sharp observation, analysis, judgement of people, creativity and the ability to synthesise disparate parts into wholes.

Over the educational objectives of the school, a more extended and continuous process of consultation and negotiation may be involved. The Head's part in this is pivotal. Among the many steps which can make up that part are the following:

1   Express personal views and findings based on, perhaps, wider experience than that of anyone else in the school.
2   Encourage staff to think about educational objectives, to express their views honestly and fearlessly, establishing and highlighting the common ground, and identifying the differences.
3   Guide the governing body in its duties under the Education Act, 1986, particularly with regard to general principles on discipline.
4   Work for overall consensus between staff and governors.
5   Apply his or her own powers of persuasion at all levels with a view to obtaining genuine conversion to and support of desirable objectives. As one Head has put it:

When I was deputy head, I had strong views about how things ought to be run. As Head now I realise how much I had miscalculated. The power of the views of the staff is real. I had expected more or less to have a one man job but I find in practice it has to be a corporate effort. But I am also finding the value of persuasion and this is fast becoming one of my most important developing arts.

With respect to resource objectives, the Head has a different kind of executive responsibility. The governors, under their legally founded and newly defined duties, will be able in future to question not only what is taught — the province of educational objectives — but how it is taught, which is the province of resource objectives. However, it is the clear responsibility of the Head, once educational objectives have been agreed, to deploy and develop all resources — the staff, space, facilities, equipment, materials, finance and time — to achieve those objectives. This is the basis of the accountability of the Head. Binding the Head's hands in this matter is a contradiction in management terms and can lead to vexation, trouble, and possible disaster. The Head needs discretion and freedom to act in conjunction with the staff and the local education authority's advisers to set resource objectives in such a way that the educational objectives can be reached.

At first sight, the province of personal objectives might seem to be outside the legitimate purview and responsibility of the Head. On the contrary, the Head has a firm part to play in them. In the first place, the Head is inextricably bound up with and influenced by his or her own personal objectives. These need to be constantly reviewed and, perhaps, justified in terms of the interests of the school.

Second, the Head in his or her capacity as professional leader may properly seek to influence the personal objectives of the members of staff, especially the teaching staff and particularly with respect to their professional development and future careers. At critical times in the life of the school when important decisions are being made, the persuasive activity of the Head in relation to the teaching staff's personal objectives could be decisive.

Third, as is expected, the Head is the key figure in the lives of the children and their parents. The Head is able to exercise influence over the personal objectives which may be adopted with regard to many issues in school work, attitudes, ambitions and out-of-school activities. This, after all, is the formal province of the work of an educator.

Critical points about objectives

As indicated above, the Head might assume different levels of responsibility and exercise different prerogatives between the three kinds of objectives. The setting of all objectives other than personal objectives, however, still needs to be regarded as a corporate matter. As far as is practicable, everyone affected by an objective should be variously subject to the following conditions:

1   they should be involved in its formulation;

2   they should be informed of its existence if not so involved;
3   they should be reminded of its existence at appropriate times;
4   they should be encouraged to reiterate it themselves;
5   they should be briefed to report on progress towards its achievement;
6   they should be invited to celebrate its achievement;
7   they should be expected to review it from time to time, with a view to retaining, modifying, removing or replacing it.

Fulfilling this corporate activity is vital to the achievement of effective management; it is easy enough, however, to overlook particular items. The Head of a small school in a village where gossip was rife chose to rotate three local women as reserve dinner ladies on the occasions when regular kitchen staff were absent. The Head did not inform the three women about the idea of rotation. Each reserve dinner lady thought that she was to be the regular reserve supply person. When the time came to give way to the third, the second woman took umbrage and created a scene in the school, claiming that she had been unfairly rejected as inadequate. Clearly, the Head was entitled to have an objective to ensure a flexible future supply of reserve kitchen staff with experience and proven worth. But conditions 1 and 2 above should have been observed prior to the commitment of the women to the job. Had these conditions been observed, an unpleasant outcome could have been avoided.

It is common to find poor 'communication' listed as a matter of concern or a problem among teachers. This can mean many things and varies from school to school. Sometimes it means the paperwork is inadequate: at other times it means that meetings are unprofitable or that split sites or distances between buildings lead to difficulties. At the heart of complaints about poor communication is more often than not a plea to be clearly informed as to what the objective is by the person responsible for making the objective or seeing that it is actually made. Whilst people often like to be involved in the making of objectives, they are frequently content not to be involved and sometimes have to be coaxed into being so involved. However, they all like to know what the objective is. Indeed they *must* be informed if the objective is to be reached. Curiously, some teachers cannot find it in themselves to state what the objective is to their colleagues. It is sometimes a reticence rooted in reservations about carrying authority and fear of negative reactions from colleagues, but sometimes it is a lack of clarity and understanding about the objective itself. So others are left to infer the objective or learn about it by hearsay and often incorrectly.

All seven conditions which need to be met in fulfilment of the corporate nature of objectives chiefly affect four bodies in the primary school — the governors, the staff, the parents and the children. They can be variously involved according to the objectives being considered. An objective set and an objective reached as a result of corporate effort require a basis of shared values. When values are shared, unity can be said to exist. Among the many disparate adults and children who make up a primary school, however, it cannot be expected that everyone concerned will agree. Indeed, it may be preferable that they should not agree. A large majority or consensus in favour of the main values is necessary, put in a form of words to which those concerned can give their assent. This should be sought primarily for the organisational mission objectives of the school. Decreasing consensus among those who are involved is likely to be found in passing from the formulation of organisational mission objectives to educational objectives and finally to resource objectives.

Unity is variable over time and over different issues. If the underlying values are sufficiently common, survival can be assured. Difficulties can be overcome and goodwill will usually prevail. But unity should not be confused with uniformity. There is no hope of having uniformity in anything, whether values, opinion or practices. Whereas unity may be seen as a desirable characteristic of the primary school, uniformity may be seen as essentially undesirable. Superficial uniformities, as in dress and procedures, are intended to enhance the unity of the school. Unity does not require uniformity and may be impossible to achieve at all if uniformity is pursued. This clearly applies to a class of heterogeneous children. It can apply also to the work of teaching staff in the school, notably to their teaching styles. The absence of uniformity of teaching styles and avoidance of suggestions that styles are either right or wrong — as distinct from being related to the educational objective — are more likely to promote unity than the opposite approach.

If the publicly required list of aims is taken into account, every primary school is able to quote what in this chapter has been defined and described as objectives. Some will be written but some will be stated verbally. In such lists of objectives, every single one of them will seem laudable and justifiable. No-one will deny that each in its own right is worth pursuing. It might be remembered, however, that an objective is formulated and stated at one point in time to feed, sustain and direct the efforts of everyone for a subsequent period of time until the objective is reached. This is the period over which perhaps many people work to translate desire and intention into action and reality. The issue here is the number of objectives which are adopted. The principle for deciding what the number ought to be is to have as few objectives as possible (this applies whenever objectives are set and to whichever kind of objectives—even one's personal objectives). This is for two reasons. First, the people involved cannot be expected to retain in their memory more than, say, three or four objectives, which are to guide them in their work. Even if they can remember them, they cannot be expected to act decisively if there are more than a small number, since, with the addition of every extra objective, moral dilemmas arise and objectives begin to inhibit each other. An individual's efforts can no longer be highly focused on one particular cause. The second reason is that an objective, as a tool of management, is meant to determine the way in which resources are used and the scale of use. The greater the number of objectives, the more the available resources are dissipated and the less likely any of the objectives is to be realised.

The efforts of staff, governors, parents and children involved in a school need to be focused on a few discrete and sharply significant objectives, which are mutually reconcilable, easy to remember, and easy to quote. Such objectives can be readily used as the touchstone for all the many events and activities that would otherwise be regarded as disparate, disconnected and without overall meaning.

Objectives need to be as few in number and as discrete in nature as possible

Objectives, once decided and formulated, need to have an appropriate time tag attached to them, an indication of the standard of result which is expected and an order of priority. If, for example, an objective is to show unfailing courtesy to all visitors to the school, the time tag is obviously 'at all times'. But if the objective is to enable every child to be proficient in the use of the computer, a date needs to be attached. This might be, for example, 'by the end of the child's third year in the junior school'. The time tag implies that sufficient computers, teaching competence, software and supplies are available. Similarly, if a resource objective is established for the complete revision of mathematics teaching, it might be framed along the lines that a teacher shall have been retrained and new books and materials bought and made ready for use by a certain date.

The standard of result expected is also important. In the case of the unfailing courtesy objective, the standard might be that shown by the typical nurse towards patients, or by an air-hostess to passengers. The standard for the computer objective might be specified in terms of the pupil's successful completion of certain programmes. A standard for the objective to modify mathematics teaching in the school might be the detailed minimum performance in areas agreed with the local secondary school and other link primary schools at fourth year junior level.

Furthermore, an order of priority needs to be attached to every objective. This may change over time. Not all objectives are important at any one time. They cannot all be served simultaneously. The time tag acts as a regulator. But above all there should be a sense of priority among objectives. Various events and conditions will cause priorities to change. For example, in one year an onslaught on unruly behaviour which has developed may be necessary. Or it may be necessary to give attention to the improvement of handwriting. When accomplished, specific dependent objectives like these give way to others clamouring for attention. All the time, however, they depend in turn on higher level objectives to give point and purpose, a sense of direction and a sense of priority. Strategy and timescale are important things to use in management if a school is not to be imprisoned by the urgency of immediate events. Dealing exclusively with the immediate can induce a loss of a sense of direction and proportion. It is useful on this score to distinguish between the timescales of short term or immediate objectives, medium term or attainable objectives, and long term or visionary objectives. Immediate objectives refer to carrying out agreed policy, keeping the school open, working within present arrangements. Attainable objectives refer to changes in resource use within the present resource limits. Visionary objectives are those which may well require additional as well as differently used resources. In effect they respectively represent what is, what could be soon and what might be in the future. In staff discussions, it is well to be clear as to which of the three kinds of timescales and objectives are under consideration. Often the busy Head is preoccupied with immediate objectives, while an enthusiastic teacher is carried away by visionary objectives. However, it commonly occurs that the Head needs to lead the staff into the realms of attainable and visionary objectives, which they are reluctant to work for because they are obsessed with immediate objectives.

In this review of the concept of objectives, the preferred focus has been on outputs or results, rather than inputs and intentions. The idea of aims has been subsumed into the single concept of objectives. The whole point of objectives, after all, is the marshalling of resources — particularly human behaviour — to obtain good results rather than mediocre or poor results.

The organisational mission objectives of the school, once set, are probably subject to little change over considerable periods of time. Educational, resource and personal objectives, however, are variously subject to change and may be volatile. Keeping a close watch on objectives is a central necessity for effective headship. From time to time the objectives should be reviewed by individuals on behalf of the school as a whole. The framework of this chapter may be used to do this, as suggested in Figure 2.3. It provides space for educational, resource and personal objectives over the short, medium and long terms. An individual can enter the objectives (as he or she understands them) in the appropriate cells of the matrix, putting them in order of priority and ensuring that they are few in number. A Head or any other member of staff could make use of the matrix with respect to his or her own range of tasks and level of responsibility.

The school's objectives might be displayed in the Head's room and/or the staff room. The chart would certainly contain the school's organisational mission and educational objectives. It might also contain the school's resource objectives. It should be possible to see from such a chart exactly where the main thrust of the school's efforts lies. To be effective, this needs to be directed towards the accomplishment of relatively few major things.

Above all, it is necessary to focus the entire efforts of the school on to

FIGURE 2.3   Matrix for reviewing objectives

Objectives as at................19

Timescale / Category	Short term (Immediate)	Medium term (Attainable)	Long term (Visionary)
Educational			
Resource			
Personal			

some realistic, worthwhile and achievable objectives. Edith Moorhouse, the 'architect' of primary education in Oxfordshire from 1946 to 1968, acted as an exemplar of this. Of her it has been said:

Looking back, her strength was her awesome simplicity. The hallmark was five or six things done really well . . . for example, children's literature and exploratory expeditions in the natural environment as the basis for classroom work[2].

The concept of results

The primary school is no exception to the rule that every organisation exists to provide planned results or outcomes. If there is any doubt about what they should be in the primary school, the following question may be asked. If this particular school did not exist, what would remain undone and who would suffer?

In the case of manufacturing organisations it is easy to see the answer to the question. The organisation's physical products — which can be measured, weighed and counted — would not appear on the market. Those who wanted them would be disappointed. The effects of their absence from the market could be trivial — as in the case of luxury or inessential goods. But they could be serious — as in the case of medical supplies or other goods crucial for the saving and preservation of life.

Service organisations, in contrast, facilitate the transactions of human life, including the circulation and distribution of goods. These have seen a spectacular growth in recent years, at the expense of manufacturing, and now employ a majority of the working population. Their product includes advice and assistance of all kinds for the successful marketing, absorption and use of manufactured goods.

A third group consists of caring organisations. They are devoted to human happiness and welfare, the relief of pain and suffering, protection and custody, reformation and rehabilitation, and the facilitation of individual purposes. Hospitals, prisons, homes and training and welfare centres are included in this group. Their product is to put people back on their feet mentally or physically, to constrain people, to train people and to provide personal satisfaction, to give advice and to give care and comfort.

Schools are not quite like any of these. They provide a little of most of the functions mentioned in the case of the care organisations. They set out to supply knowledge and skills training but these are also part of the work of manufacturing, service and care organisations, either for their clients or for their own workforce. Schools are unique in having the task of helping young people to come to terms with themselves and the world in which they find themselves, to have a sense of purpose and direction in it and to acquire the means to achieve that purpose in preparing for adulthood and citizenship.

Unique though the results or outcomes of this work may be, the primary school can have its own measures of performance or ways of gauging it. It needs to be recognised that results or work done has two aspects. It may first be considered with regard to its *quantity*. It may also be considered with regard to its *quality*. Usually one is achieved at the expense of the other. If resources are held at the same level, the quantity of work done can be increased only at the expense of its quality. Conversely, quality can only be increased at the expense of quantity if resources are held at the same level. But not everything needs to be done to the same high quality standards. For some things, this is a waste of resources. Where quality *is* necessary, however, it requires more resources. This is the broad argument behind staff development. Unless teachers move with the times, keeping up to date with knowledge and its associated teaching methods, the quality of the teaching they provide is likely to decline.

Staffing, however, is an expensive resource and retraining or updating to maintain or improve quality levels can be prohibitive. Literally everything that takes place within school hours, or is sponsored or directed by the school but takes place outside of school hours, counts as results. They include what is going on generally as well as specific achievements which can be measured more or less precisely. Results can include, by association, anything of note achieved by staff or children in their private lives as hobbies or interests. Results in this sense contribute to the final product — the effect on the child, which may be temporary or lasting.

The public image of the school is affected positively if a teacher or a pupil makes laudable headlines and negatively if the headlines are unworthy. The following list is a miscellany of potential headlines which illustrates the range of items that can be covered by the inclusive concept of results. Any of them could appear in the press or simply be pointed up and given visibility by the school in other ways.

- children praised for their work with old people
- instances of parental praise for the school
- number of hours spent on mathematics
- school wins children's business enterprise scheme award
- children's expressions of happiness at being at school
- children's work on display
- teacher completes a half marathon for charity
- school football team tops the league
- computers introduced into the curriculum
- music and drama enjoyed by parents
- Head publishes a class book on craft, design and technology
- school hall repainted by parents at their own expense
- new netball goal posts installed
- two school journeys — one at home, one abroad
- school becomes showpiece for its language work
- science work doubled throughout the curriculum
- newly designed school brochure
- outstanding pottery from the newly installed kiln
- school's average reading age raised

Each of these disparate items in its own way acts as a performance indicator of the school. Some are concerned with resource inputs — the computers have arrived (but nothing has yet been done with them). Some are concerned with precise quality outputs — the average reading age score has been raised. Some are highly subjective in nature — the opinions of parents, for example. Some are objective in nature, such as the time spent on mathematics and science. In general, however, they are all concerned with the present and the immediate future. The list might be importantly and additionally fortified by including items which reflect the long term work of the school. Such items could be, for instance,

- former pupil returns to her own primary school as teacher
- overseas visitor returns to see his old primary school

The work output or results of the primary school may be viewed inclusively. Increasing pressure is being applied on schools to produce and publish results in a form which is quantifiable, auditable and will permit comparisons between schools and with performance levels of previous years within the same school. These can typically be cast in terms of numbers of pupils, financial costs and attainment levels in knowledge and skills in various subject fields. It is not necessary to be able to measure the product of the school in strictly quantitative terms in order to have results. Some can be quantified but many cannot be. To be an effective school, however, there must be a reckoning of what has been achieved, what the product is over a period of time. Being alert to what is going on, and what the school's work and influence in extended form is and can become, is characteristic of the effective Head. If there are plenty of results, publicity should take care of itself, but, in addition, the deliberate action of the Head or designated member of staff in giving the school sustained publicity may be no bad thing. Figure 2.4 could be used to record results for purposes of reports, publicity and meetings.

FIGURE 2.4   Performance indicators/production chart for the primary
school

Pupils' achievements

Individual achievements in school
- academic
- practical
- creative

Individual achievements out of school
- academic
- practical
- creative

Aggregate achievements in school
- standardised scores
- other

Aggregate achievements out of school
- activities
- competitions

Buildings Modifications, maintenance, improvements in their use.

FIGURE 2.4 (*Continued*)

Materials and equipment New acquisitions, new use

Communications to the school on its work from outside

Pupils' conduct
Trends in
- lateness
- absence
- truancy
- misbehaviour in class
- vandalism
- crime
- health

Curriculum
   Analysis of hours spent per subject/area over the year
   Changes completed, started and being implemented

School events
   Projects completed, started and being implemented

Staff
Individual achievements
- additional qualifications, appointments
- publications
- out of school honours, awards, activities

Aggregate achievements
- INSET hours for the year
- status factors, eg number of graduate staff
- competence factors, eg all staff able to use computer

Relating the key concepts

The three managerial concepts of resources, objectives and results have been brought together in this chapter. Resources can be marshalled and put to use in an orderly, purposeful and controlled way by the proper use of objectives, which indicate the intended results. Performance is a record of those results, viewed in retrospect. This, in brief, is what management is about. In a general management capacity, the Head undertakes this function at school level. His or her effectiveness is judged accordingly.

Good management in the primary school is a matter of achieving exceptional results (performance) with unexceptional resources, particularly when this happens in unpropitious circumstances. Towards effective

management, the vital concepts of this chapter may be put together as
follows:

Management = (resources ◀────▶ objectives) ────▶ results/outcomes

where management is what is needed to relate available resources to feasible
objectives to produce the desired results.

3

Exercising leadership

It is often said that the important thing to know about a primary school is who is in charge. As a matter of formality, of course, the Head is in charge and everyone expects this to be so in practice. It is unfortunate if, in reality, the Head is not in charge. If someone else has usurped the leadership, it can have unpleasant consequences for the well-being and effectiveness of the school.

It is not enough, however, to ask who is in charge. An equally vital question to ask is *how* that person is in charge. This chapter is about exercising leadership, which consists of these two parts: having and keeping the leadership, together with the manner or style in which it is exercised. The two must go hand in hand. Too often in the past leadership has been regarded as an indivisible behavioural characteristic, with the assumption that a person either has it or does not have it. Those who are supposed not to have it have frequently been discounted simply because they did not exhibit a particular style of leadership which in the minds of others was all that leadership could ever be. Usually this has been associated with so called 'masculine' qualities, especially tough, determined, hard-hitting and dictatorial forms of behaviour. In education, many have thought of leadership like this as belonging to the military or to business: it could have no place in schools, particularly in primary schools. In truth, modern leadership is not conceived of as being like that in the armed forces or in the commercial world. But leadership of an appropriate style is required — indeed, it is unavoidable — in all organisations if they intend to be effective, not least the primary school.

The case for leadership

Leadership is expected of the Head of the primary school. It is not an option. In one sense, the Head, once appointed, cannot help being the leader. The aura and title of leader are conferred formally by the office held. Leadership is the making of the path along which others are prepared to follow for one reason or another. The Head is in the best position to be leader. As general manager and titular head of the school, the Head is leader by definition in the first instance. In terms of creating a path and persuading others to follow along it, however, others may also become leaders.

Those with no formal management position can exercise leadership. This might even develop into opposition to the Head and create divergent directions for others to follow. For the sake of unity and good order in the school, the Head's own overall leadership needs to prevail. This is not to imply that the Head's views and judgements are always right and in the best interests of the school. It does not imply either that the leadership of others will necessarily be detrimental to the school or that it is motivated by unworthy considerations. Working with the Head means that others need to modulate their own leadership. For the Head's part, the potential leadership in others needs to be put to constructive use. The management of special projects for the school may be delegated for such purposes. In this way talents are developed for the good of the school as part of an overall and controlled programme. The individuals concerned can ease any frustrations they may have by experiencing the satisfaction of achieving something special and getting results.

The leadership of a primary school is a visible and powerful variable. It is expressed in a thousand ways. To the eye of the trained and experienced observer or practised professional, it can be detected in and through quite minor matters and events which would escape the notice of the casual caller — or at least would seem to be without significance. By noting the kind of leadership, teachers themselves can often infer as much about life and work in someone else's school as the staff in that school can tell them.

The kind of leadership exhibited is in one sense value free in that no specific kind of leadership, however categorised and defined, can claim to have such intrinsic merit that everyone feels compelled to hold it in automatic and unquestionable esteem. The leadership in one school is different from that of another because the values cherished are different — or at least are given a different order of priority. One school, for example, may value uniformity, conformity and orthodoxy; another may, in contrast, value heterogeneity, eccentricity and heterodoxy. One school may prefer order and simplicity to muddle and complexity, but another the reverse.

Leadership towards different ends can be supplemented by leadership towards different means by which to achieve those ends. The means by which valued ends are pursued are themselves subject to differing valuations. One school will establish order by one set of means; another will do so by the use of a quite different set. In the case of achieving a major reform of the curriculum, one school will attain the reform by a set of means which is diametrically opposite in character to that adopted by another school attempting to reach the same outcome.

Since leadership, above all, means the implicit or explicit assertion of values, certain individuals in schools will always seek to have the ascendancy over others and expect to be able to do so. This is an important point of distinction in the primary school between teaching staff and non-teaching staff and between teachers and children. As a basis for distinction between teaching staff and parents, however, it has weakened. Parents are more able now to project their own values in the school. Nevertheless, certain members of the teaching staff, the Head above all, have decisive work to do to synthesise and crystallise values — if not to impose them. Their positions, salaries and standing are for masterminding the values held. Mutually contradictory and clearly unacceptable values, brought into the school through children and parents, have to be accommodated. This may imply compromise or the superimposition of the school's corporate values.

The Head's leadership of the school starts with the first steps taken and ends with the ultimate establishment of the recognised and characteristic way in which the school is run and for which it becomes known. The leadership of each and every other senior member of staff needs also to be achieved in its own sphere. By such leadership the ethos and climate is created within which staff and children make their commitments and devote their best efforts to the school.

Leadership style

The Head may give a great deal of thought to how he or she is prepared at any time to go about things. The emerging pattern created by such choices is the leadership style. In colloquial speech leadership style is encapsulated in phrases such as 'like a bull in a china shop' or 'playing the waiting game', which abound in everyday use. Some of the ingredients which make up the Head's preferred ways of acting are subject to little or no control by the person concerned. These are notably physical attributes such as height, bearing and facial features. Even so, some physical attributes can be changed by practice or at will. Consciously making an effort to smile, varying the pitch of the voice and modifying standing and walking habits are obvious examples.

Other ingredients which make up a person's preferred behaviour are clearly subject to his or her own control. Among the most important of these are knowledge — of self, of others, of the job, of the situation and of management — and the choice of objectives and outcomes which are sought. Chosen ways of going about things can be enormously varied. In all cases, however, they amount to the same considerations in the end. These are caring about the work which has to be accomplished and caring about the people who have to do it.

Figure 3.1 is a framework of the choices of leadership style within which the primary school Head can work. The vertical axis is a psychological dimension of leadership. At one extreme is the self-effacing Head, leading from behind, facilitating the work of others and putting them at the centre of everything that is happening. He or she is constrained in

FIGURE 3.1 Leadership style choices

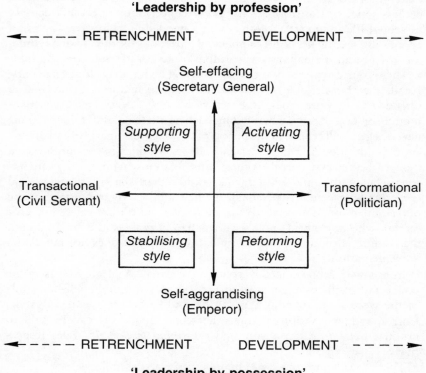

'**Leadership by profession**'

◄ − − − −− RETRENCHMENT   DEVELOPMENT − − − − −►

Self-effacing
(Secretary General)

| Supporting style | Activating style |

Transactional
(Civil Servant)

Transformational
(Politician)

| Stabilising style | Reforming style |

Self-aggrandising
(Emperor)

◄ − − − − − RETRENCHMENT   DEVELOPMENT − − − − −►

'**Leadership by possession**'

behaviour and is not anxious for personal prominence and honours as a way of competing with colleagues. The corporate nature of the school features low power and authority differentials, with the Head as its symbol, servant and agent. At the other extreme of the psychological dimension is the self-aggrandising Head, leading from the front and in the centre of everything that is happening. He or she retains a strong sense of competition for prominence and honours among close colleagues. The corporate nature of the school is achieved by high power and authority differentials. The Head is the director and prime mover, frequently exhibiting great charisma.

In contrast, the horizontal axis is a work dimension of leadership. At one extreme is the Head who views the work of headship as an endless series of transactions. They are not without their excitement but are best dealt with dispassionately. The parameters for doing so are set by precedent. Proven practice is the status quo. Inevitably there are pressures or directives from outside which compel changes but the watchword is to avoid disturbance as much as possible. This particularly applies to the handling of forces for change arising from within the school. At the other extreme of the work dimension is the Head who views headship as an endless series of transformations. Every conceivable aspect and activity of school life is subject to enthusiastic remodelling. Modernisation and adaptation are the keynotes of policy. Restrictions on the use of anything are absent and the hallmark is freedom of action for individuals.

These four categories — the self-effacing Head, the self-aggrandising Head, the transactional Head and the transformational Head — are intended to be pure types. In practice, however, every Head can place himself or herself somewhere along each of the two dimensions. Some, nevertheless, will represent the pure types rather more sharply than others. As the sub-titles in Figure 3.1 indicate, some Heads are more like a modern Secretary-General of the United Nations, whose role is impersonal, facilitative and self-effacing, rather than that of the historical emperor, whose rule is personal, explicit and self-aggrandising. In the other dimension, some Heads are more like the traditional senior civil servant who implements policy rather than originates it, compared with the traditional politician who originates policy but does not handle its implementation.

In this way four leadership styles are created. A Head who is in the upper half of the psychological or vertical axis and in the left-hand side of the work or horizontal axis can be said to have a *supporting* style. Corresponding positions in the other three quadrants can be said to produce *activating, stabilising* and *reforming leadership* styles respectively.

These four leadership styles may be described as follows.

Supporting style

Tending to be self-effacing as a person and transactional in the conduct of work. Using deferential rule and leading from behind. Managing the school in an orderly and systematic way along conventional lines.

A teacher's view of the supporting style:

The Head is so kind and considerate. She takes a real interest in my work and always has a word of praise and encouragement. She doesn't impose her own ideas but brings out my own and regularly invites my opinion on things that are happening in the school. Everything here is in good order and the school works well. She is on top of the work of keeping the school going but . . . she literally doesn't work hard enough . . . I mean she doesn't look out enough for what ought to be happening — where the school ought to be going, what we should be doing differently.

Activating style

Tending to be self-effacing as a person and transformational in the conduct of work. Using deferential rule and leading from behind. Managing the school by initiating changes and ongoing experiment.

A teacher's view of the activating style:

The new Head found our school to be a bit of a backwater. It had a bad reputation. The teaching was formal: the display work was weak. The staff were elderly and didn't feel like a team. Parents didn't help the school. The children were under-motivated and had short attention spans. The governors were nice people, not distinguished, and were uninvolved in the school.

When the new Head arrived she was quiet and courteous. She didn't seem to do much at first. We began to wonder if the school was doomed. Then one by one things began to happen. One teacher who was a worrier and very elderly was redeployed in favour of a youngster with bags of energy. The Head helped the scale post teacher responsible for display work in the school to make a fresh start.

She talked to us about our teaching methods and made us all feel it was worth making an effort. It was so unassuming — no pressure, no bullying. We suddenly saw governors in the school during the day and got a piece of good news in the local paper. Before long we began to realise we were working more as a team. Eventually the Head drew our attention to the low levels of motivation and concentration of the children — a serious problem that really did need tackling. Looking back now so much has changed but we hardly knew it was happening at the time.

Stabilising style

Tending to be self-aggrandising as a person and transactional in the conduct of work. Using autocratic rule and leading from the front. Managing the school in an orderly and systematic way along conventional lines.

A teacher's view of the stabilising style:

I have been teaching in this school for seven years. All this time I have been taking first-year juniors. Each year I teach the same thing at about the same time. For example, in history I have to teach the Romans and in mathematics I have to teach long division. In both these cases the Head has told me what I must teach and how it is to be done. I have begged him to let me have a change of teaching — with, say, second-year juniors but he won't listen. I have tried several times to get him to let me change the programme of teaching for first-year juniors but, again, he won't let me do it. Things are too settled. It's time that the school had a good shake-up.

Reforming style

Tending to be self-aggrandising as a person and transformational in the conduct of work. Using autocratic rule and leading from the front. Managing the school by pressing through changes and directing continual experiment.

A teacher's view of the reforming style:

Under the previous Head the school had become really run down. The staff were not allowed to discuss issues concerning the school. Staff meetings were for information only. The Head and staff were alienated from one another and the climate in the school was poor. Some things had become neglected — there was no staff handbook, requests for action over a reading problem from the nearby secondary school were disregarded, and we were estranged from the infant school which is on the same site. There were cliques in the staffroom and everyone taught in isolation from the rest. Curriculum documents were unheard of. It's nice to be free from upset in a school and to know where you are but in this school it was quietness to the point of death.

The new Head changed all that. He shook us up with great gusto. He got us working on the curriculum and a staff handbook, invited staff discussions, went out of his way to make good relations with other schools, changed the reading scheme and got us all working together. It was like a breath of fresh air — or rather a gale. Nothing seemed to be able to stand in his way and he led it all.

The main difference between the four leadership styles is made explicit in Figure 3.1. It may be seen in the model that the school is constantly suspended between undergoing *retrenchment* (on the left-hand side) and undergoing *development* (marked on the right-hand side). The Head, in his or her own way — depicted here by the contrasting *supporting* and *stabilising* styles — can lead the school into greater calm and reflection. On the other hand the Head, again in his or her own way — depicted here by the contrasting *activating* and *reforming* styles — can lead the school into greater activity and change.

The choice of direction and the rate at which movement occurs calls for good judgement. But it cannot be overemphasised that such a movement is not to be conceived as a once-for-all event. Effective headship is dominated by the need to exercise good judgement all the time over which direction to take but, in addition, how long to stay in retrenchment or development before correcting the balance again.

Finally, in Figure 3.1, it may be seen that recognition is given to the more corporate form of leadership — depicted as 'leadership by profession' and represented by the *supporting* and *activating* styles. In contrast is the more personalised form of leadership — depicted as 'leadership by possession' and represented by the *stabilising* and *reforming* styles. Both forms of leadership are legitimate.

Variable leadership

It may be inferred from Figure 3.1 that there is no outright 'best buy'. There are different kinds of leadership, each of which can be successful in appropriate circumstances. Some teachers prefer one kind of leadership, others a different kind. The leadership of the Head is of the school as a whole, creating the climate and conditions within which everyone can give of his or her best. The particular style of leadership chosen must be capable of conveying a simultaneous and high concern both for the work to be done and for the people doing it. It becomes reflected in the movements of mood, the direction and levels of activity, and the standards of work and conduct achieved over long periods of time.

In the life cycle of the primary school different kinds of leadership are needed at different times. On the occasions when a new Head is being appointed, it is the foremost responsibility of the governing body, and others concerned with the appointment, to judge very carefully the kind of leadership which is needed and to appoint someone who is capable of giving it.

However, the opportunity to reappraise the needs of the school and to appoint a new Head accordingly occurs relatively rarely. In the absence of limited contracts for Heads, a school may be subject to the leadership of the same Head for many years. During such a period the needs of the school are likely to vary and to call for significant modifications in the kind of leadership needed. In the future, as seldom before, uncertain and sometimes volatile conditions for adaptation and survival will put a premium on leadership in the primary school. The demands of the legislation in recent Education Acts will play no small part in this. The pressure is on each Head to be capable of varying his or her leadership to cope with changing conditions and needs within the period of his or her headship of the same school. It may be necessary, for example, for a new Head — having assessed the situation on appointment — to be the reforming leader to correct a long period of stagnation and indifferent performance. Following the successful survival of the school, he or she may then have to offer a period of stabilising leadership to consolidate the gains, pausing for reflection and reinforcing the learning which has taken place. In both these cases self-assertive leadership may well be needed.

In contrast, a new Head may have to act exactly in reverse if conditions are opposite, however tempting it may be to make a mark with a dramatic innovation or other evidence of his or her accession to the headship. This may be the case if the previous Head has left behind a welter of unfinished or aborted changes, or if the school has suffered a scandal or other seriously disruptive event such as a fire.

Prevailing conditions in the school may require activating leadership followed by supportive leadership, or the reverse. In more extreme conditions, the Head may actually need to cross the divide between leadership by profession and leadership by possession. It is suggested that changing from one of these to the other at any time is justified according to the prevailing attitudes and conduct of staff, children and parents, governors, and the external forces which have to be satisfied.

Prominent individuals may exhibit unrestrained behaviour intended to sabotage measures designed thoroughly and objectively for the improvement of the school. They may work actively, if clandestinely, to create schism in the sentiment and co-operation of the staff or parents. In cases like this leadership by possession is likely to be needed. Insofar as prevailing attitudes and conduct are restrained in a line towards constructive thought and criticism and the generation of corporate sentiment and effort, leadership by profession is more likely to be needed.

It is impossible to be effective as a Head without leadership. That given, the focus is then on the kind or style of leadership which is offered. Leadership needs to be conceived not as strong or weak or indifferent leadership but in terms of clarity and the choice of style, judged by its degree of suitability for the situation. It is unlikely that any single style will meet all circumstances, suit all people and achieve all that might be achieved. Accepting this is probably a step towards wisdom: not accepting it is probably the chief cause for an earnest and hardworking Head's efforts coming to a standstill. Deflection from the necessary leadership style leads to the disintegration of leadership itself.

Clearly, the timescale involved in this issue is important. In the short run mistakes might be made but these can be corrected successfully. The early period of headship sees the build-up of a particular leadership style. It is over the longer period, however, that more fundamental changes in the needs of the school may require a significant and subtle change of style. If in post for many years, an effective Head is the sophisticated leader who is able to vary his or her leadership style according to strategic need. In other words there is a time for the exercise of supporting, activating, stabilising and reforming styles according to need.

However, few people are likely to be masters of their own behaviour to the point of being able to exercise every style to perfection. On the other hand, rigidity of style, carried over into inappropriate circumstances from times when it was clearly the appropriate style, is undesirable. Everyone can achieve some flexibility and become more effective in so doing: rigidity may indicate fatigue and exhaustion.

A potential handicap in achieving a flexible leadership style might be the individual's beliefs about what is the best style for a Head to use. Furthermore, it is possible that a Head could have a fixed self-image with regard to the style of which he or she believes himself or herself to be capable. A Head said the following, on taking up her second headship:

I find this school rather different from the previous one. It is something of a challenge. The staff have been used to autocracy but I am no autocrat. However, I think we are beginning to understand each other. The children come from varied backgrounds with a surprising number of problems. They are very pleasant and friendly, though, as are the parents and governors.

In using the terms 'autocracy' and 'autocrat' — irrespective of what she meant by them — the Head was clearly referring to leadership style. She did not necessarily disapprove of a style which she called 'autocracy' but one inference may be drawn: that whatever it consisted of she believed she could not produce it. The second inference which may be drawn is that, even if she could produce an autocratic style, she would not choose to do so. This may have been on account of what she thought was right or what was in vogue. She evidently did not reflect that the previous Head may have wished to do otherwise but exhibited 'autocracy' because it was the leadership style thought to be necessary at that time. She implies, perhaps, that her predecessor was a one-style Head, but equally that her own leadership style in the end could prove as inflexible. There is insufficient evidence to know whether the one style or the other is suitable for the school, though the new Head is clearly aware of the impact a chosen style can make, particularly if it sharply contrasts with that of her predecessor.

Should any Head have reservations about being able to exercise flexibility in leadership style, he or she might reflect on the fact that a good teacher precisely exhibits such a skill in managing a class of children. Changes in style take place on a short-cycle basis sometimes within and often between class sessions. But more importantly, it can take place on a long-cycle basis over a term or whole school year as part of a well thought out control strategy. It is the latter which can serve as a model for flexible leadership style for the school as a whole.

The effective Head is one who can vary his or her leadership style as required by the changing needs of the school over a longer period of time

Grounds of leadership

The Head's leadership has every chance of prevailing, provided that he or she is aware of the automatic advantages which go with appointment and handles them prudently. Initially, everything is in the Head's favour for being able to establish and exercise the leadership of the school. It can continue unabated, provided that he or she can avoid ill-conceived actions and thoughtless behaviour which compromises or even discredits his or her standing.

On appointment the Head enjoys the traditional authority which society and the profession attach to headship and which they expect the Head to be able to use. This is transferred from the previous Head and originates with the employer as appointing body. Once in post and with a track record to his or her credit, the Head can acquire the additional authority which is conferred by those who make up the school. This comes from the recognition and respect of staff, parents and children, and the governors. It is now based on *wanting* to follow because of a good track record, rather than on being obliged to follow as at the outset.

The possession of authority can be a snare and a trap for the unwary. It may inflate the ego of its possessor, yet induce complacency and inactivity equally as much as self-projection and hyperactivity. Learning to handle authority is a tricky step for deputy heads to take when assuming their first headships. The Head of a primary school needs to preserve the vital and distinctive qualities which mark out the good primary teacher while taking up the general management task. The difficulty of doing this is captured by such sayings as 'a man or woman with ideas has no authority — a man or woman with authority has no ideas' (Thailand) and 'authority corrupts — absolute authority corrupts absolutely' (Britain).

The main ground for the Head's authority is the legal duty to control the internal organisation and discipline of the school, as stated in the *Articles of Government* of each school. The Head is accountable for this authority to several constituencies — children, staff, parents and governors — and ultimately to the local education authority (if the school is in the maintained sector) which itself has legal obligations towards the school as defined by the Education Act of 1944 and subsequent acts.

Further grounds for the Head's leadership to prevail may be found in the Head's access to and disposal of school monies. Discretion over finance is an important back-up to the Head's legal standing. The exercise of financial control has two main aspects. Finance can be allocated to stimulate new initiatives which the Head favours and to encourage existing ones which the Head prefers. Finance may be denied in order to discourage new initiatives and to terminate existing ones. Whilst the objective merits or demerits of an initiative may normally be all that is at stake, it not infrequently happens that internal political considerations need to be taken into account. The standing of particular individuals may need to be enhanced or curbed by the granting or withholding of monies, with reference to the Head's need to retain his or her leadership of the school.

Beyond the legal and financial grounds lies one more important ground of leadership. This is referential power over job prospects. The Head presides over promotional prospects of staff to a considerable degree. He or she also has the power to influence certain outcomes for children and their parents as they pass out of the primary school, particularly to other primary or secondary schools. This power of reference on behalf of staff or pupils can be decisive.

How these three powers — legal, financial and referential — are lived with and used by the Head distinguishes between the effective and the ineffective Head. They are essentially coercive in nature. If used sparingly, they can help to retain the leadership when the Head is under pressure or threat. If too much is made of them, inauthentic behaviour will almost certainly be induced in teachers, children and parents — at the extreme to a point of servility which goes well beyond the normal requirements of civil conduct. The climate of defensiveness, formality and even fear which can be produced by this would be detrimental to the spirit and work needed in the primary school. The effective Head makes it plain that the intimidating or malevolent use of these powers is not in keeping with the kind of school he or she wishes to run.

These three are indeed the hard grounds of the Head's leadership. There are, however, far more attractive and persuasive additional grounds on which the Head's leadership may be built — namely technical competence, interpersonal competence and decisional competence.

Technical competence in leadership

Technical competence in the Head is displayed as knowledge of teaching itself, knowledge of the profession of teaching, knowledge of the wider education service and the workings of the particular local education authority, and knowledge of particular subjects. It is also displayed by way of personal acumen and stature. A Head ought to be someone whose qualities are up to the job and command respect. Such qualities may be variously analysed. Those listed below are chosen because they are seen as germane to being technically competent and are attributes which are required in the discipline needed by the Head to exercise leadership.

1   Living with unfinished business
Management work is always at various stages of being 'in progress'. It is not the kind of work which has a clean start and a neat finish. It is hard, if not impossible, to lock the door on it as is possible with so many other jobs — including, in fact, many teaching jobs. Some people only seem able to 'leave work behind' and relax if it has been completed. Yet the nature of headship work is such that the idea of being able to complete work is at best relative. The Head needs to be able to grow accustomed to living with constantly unfinished business and to develop a certain detachment in order to preserve his or her mental and physical energy and to maintain a process of personal renewal.

2   Taking nothing for granted
Boundaries to what is possible are assumed in everything we do. Some are assumed to be more impervious than others. Whilst they act to bring a necessary degree of social order and predictability into the task of running schools, they can also offer barriers to the solution of problems and the development of the school. The effective Head is one who examines his or her own assumptions about boundaries and probes into those held by others, with a view to challenging or ignoring a boundary as seems necessary for the good of the school.

3   Coping with unexceptional resources
Both human and physical resources are always in various states of imperfect readiness for the job they have to do. Coping with a quality range is a constant factor in the life of the Head as general manager. It is pointless to deplore the need to do this and to dwell on what ought to

be. It is healthy, and thoroughly in the tradition of professional management, to concentrate on what can be done with what there is, whilst seeking to improve the potential of the resources to hand.

4   Facing up to adverse circumstances

The Head who is only able to be humorous, cheerful, enthusiastic and in a state of high morale when everything is going well is not likely to be an effective Head. These qualities — especially the retention of a sense of humour — are also needed when the going is rough. Others look to the Head for inspiration in such times. Leadership, in part, is helping to see others through difficult times. Being able to do this implies two things. The Head needs to know how to live with problems and enjoy the process of solving them. But in doing this he or she needs to have enough emotional strength and coping counsel left over to give to others.

5   Bearing the anger and hostility of others

The Head is the natural and automatic focus for the reactions to school life of many people. Sometimes these reactions are complimentary, sometimes they are negative and may even be pathological. Staff, children, parents and others variously feel the need to speak or write to the Head. Often this is for therapeutic purposes, to release their anxieties. The Head may regard such approaches when they are negative as a chore, a threat and an impediment. It is true that as an indicator of the state of the school it is better to have a balance of reactions in favour of the positive. Nevertheless, there will always be the negative ones and these should be regarded as an important source of information. Dealing with negative, even destructive, behaviour needs to be seen as an important professional function. It should be discharged with equanimity, understanding, sympathy and a certain detachment that remains humane and is the product of personal discipline.

6   Taking criticism

It is a common experience in organisations for senior staff to receive only filtered information from their subordinates. They are told only what others want them to hear. The management style adopted by the senior staff is probably the main reason for this. In other words, it is open to the Head in the primary school not to encourage filtered information but to create a climate, by his or her own manner and attitude, in which a free flow of information can take place. An inescapable element in such a free flow is comment about conditions and policy which may include criticism of the Head. Being able to give and take criticism without hostility is an art form. It can be learned. It can be demonstrated in private between Head and a member of staff as well as in public and in staff or parent meetings. A sense of self-importance rather than humility is the enemy of free-flowing information.

7   Accepting the contribution of others

Teachers frequently gain promotion by showing just how much they can take upon themselves. They earn a reputation of being hardworking, willing and effective. It is often an essentially individualistic progress through the profession. On becoming Heads they accomplish much, with great skill and effort. However, a residual effect of the climb to headship can be difficulty in cultivating corporate effort, which means stimulating and warmly accepting the contributions of others. Innate rivalry may linger. A performance by a member of staff which in concept, design and discharge is superior to the Head's own ability may be hard to take. Yet it is precisely the function of the effective Head to bring to full fruition all the potential that exists in staff members.

8   Working ahead of time

There is a constant torrent of jobs to be done in managing the primary school, all seeming to call for immediate if not urgent treatment. It is easy to be beguiled into thinking that keeping abreast of all these jobs is all that is required. However, room needs to be created in the Head's mind and in his or her schedule for thinking about things that have not yet appeared and for actually generating new things to think about, particularly the future development of the school. If a Head is always working up against deadlines there is almost certainly a case for reviewing his or her management of time and use of delegation. Working ahead of time is part of the discipline of management. It is not easy to achieve but it can be learned and is essential for long term effectiveness.

9   Renewing one's energy and application

The Head needs to be able to keep up the mental and physical output needed to maintain the consistent good management of the school. The Head can also provide an example to others of how to achieve personal and professional renewal, bringing untold benefits to the school. The cycle of enthusiasm followed by fatigue needs to be studied more closely in every school. There is plenty of scope for exploring how to lengthen the cycle. This is a fruitful avenue of leadership for the Head.

10   Taking risks

What seems to be a risk to one Head may not seem so to another. Some are able to see chains of logic and the development of circumstances which others cannot see. Some have more confidence in their powers and ability to see something through than others. Even so, at the margin of everyone's powers, logical reasoning and foresight, there will always be the case where the outcome is a gamble. It is foolish to run grave risks and to run too many slight risks. Yet risk-taking is part of life and is a feature of school leadership. To be afraid of taking risks is an impairment to headship. To be able to judge a good risk is an asset. It is unlikely that a Head could be effective without having taken some risks.

Interpersonal competence in leadership

Being at ease with one's colleagues and, in turn, being able to put others at their ease are skills that probably most people want to have but few exercise really well. They are inestimable assets for any Head to possess. Teaching, however, does not lend itself as fully as most other professions to the practice and cultivation of these skills with other adults. For all but a relatively small part of each working day a teacher is relating to children who are essentially dependent, immature and subject to compulsory attendance. The teacher's behavioural strategies are attuned and directed to managing the work and conduct of children in large groups. Becoming good at doing this is the object of every teacher's efforts. But in achieving the objective, the teacher may find that the long years of habituation to the task have left their mark. The years of working life spent in teaching children are at the expense of not working constantly with adults, particularly one's peers. Furthermore, it has been policy in some schools to isolate teaching staff as individuals from parents or others as far as possible in the course of school business.

Fortunately, in many primary schools the close working proximity of staff, the active encouragement of co-operative teaching and the high levels of participative involvement of the teaching staff in the general management of the school, provide opportunities to mitigate the negative efforts of not working with peers in the normal course of the working day. Parents, governors and others who come into the school on business are different in that most of them have to accommodate to their peers as a regular feature of their work.

Teachers, therefore, can be at a disadvantage in arriving at headship since they may have had insufficient experience in conducting and sustaining in-depth working relations with their peers. Natural personality, a rich out-of-school social life and the gregariousness found among so many teachers usually provide adequate compensation. In particular, the professional behavioural strategies for coping with the educational tasks during work with the children — such as a sense of humour — can be transferred to inter-adult relations in many cases. Nevertheless, some Heads find it difficult to establish good interpersonal relations with their colleagues. The range of difficulty can run from being unable to be anything other than over-complimentary to a member of staff to being terrified of a small phalanx of elderly teachers.

Interpersonal relations take place at two levels. The more visible of the two and the more superficial is the level of good company, small-talk, wit and affability. This level is important since it creates a pleasantly relaxed atmosphere. But it is not essential and without the second level it could mark a Head as being shallow in interpersonal relations.

The second level is concerned with leadership. It bestows confidence in the Head as a person of consistency and quality. To fulfil this level the Head must be predictable in his or her values and conduct. Staff should know how the Head thinks and feels to the extent of being able to anticipate the Head's reaction to a new issue. Arbitrary and devious behaviour is not advisable. Security goes with predictability and staff can learn to work constructively with it. All the time the Head should conceive 'greater' or 'higher' values over every issue. This is to raise the sights of staff and lock purposes and activities into integrated wholes. The Head should reiterate the school's values lucidly, persuasively and often.

An important thing to stress is that commitments are voluntary in the making but obligatory in the keeping. People are commonly starters of projects but uncommonly finishers of projects. This is related to the need to have a keen awareness of rights and obligations. Everyone has both. They need to balance one another. The political aspect of interpersonal relations demands the use of this formula as an invaluable tool.

Showing that colleagues can express themselves openly with impunity is an additional element at the second level. This helps to create a climate in which differences can be entertained, expressed and reconciled as a creative dynamic for the school. Above all, the Head should remain consistent with his or her own philosophy. This is the element of integrity which may inspire differences of views but at the same time generates respect.

Second-level attributes coupled with first level skills provide a sound base for interpersonal relations between the Head and individuals. But the second-level attributes are strategically essential for relations between the Head and groups or coalitions. With a small staff of, say, three or four teachers the field for the application of interpersonal relations is limited. The Head may be dealing with three or four different viewpoints which may or may not be reconcilable. With larger staffs, groupings or coalitions can develop, each expressing a different set of views, often in opposition to one another. Across the spectrum of political life of the whole school, the staff may form one such coalition, the governors a second, and the parents a third. In handling these circumstances the political skills of the Head are called for — posing one view alongside another, effecting compromises, being able to persuade, making keepable promises, being patient and having a keen sense of timing. These skills need to be exercised on the basis of second-level attributes so that the Head's interpersonal relations with groups also serve to enhance his or her leadership of the school.

The leadership derived from the Head's competence in interpersonal relations both with individuals and with groups should make it possible to get the changes which the school needs. Starting a change is relatively easy but getting it fully implemented and effectively operating requires a high degree of consensus and co-operation. This is the province of good leadership. Signs of faltering, indetermination or refusal may have to be confronted. Many innovations have foundered at the point at which the

Head as leader has failed to put his or her foot down, in the mistaken belief that interpersonal relations must always be uncontroversial and harmonious.

Decisional competence in leadership

One of the hallmarks of good leadership is the ability to take decisions. This ability is much admired by teachers but often taken for granted. The Head who can take decisions is usually thereby able to create a climate of confidence and security. In contrast, anxiety and discontent can soon be generated by the Head who is eventually seen as being unable to take decisions, as illustrated in the following case.

He had been and still was an outstanding classroom teacher with a reputation for perfectionism. On becoming deputy head he continued to teach at a very high level of effectiveness and was regarded as an example to all the staff. At the age of 35 he was promoted to his first headship but found it hard to be a teaching Head. His chief difficulty was that he found it almost impossible to take decisions. Decisions that needed to be taken were badly delayed. Sometimes, when he took a decision he would quickly change his mind, going first in one direction and then in another. This became so pronounced that the staff finally fell into a state of apathy and low morale. Curriculum development became neglected and resources became under-used. Within one year he had a break-down, which forced him to resign from his headship post and, on his recovery, to return to a classroom teaching appointment.

At the other extreme to the Head in this case are those who seem to want to decide everything within range. Clearly, the urge to make decisions as individuals and the ability to take decisions as Head varies between people and seems to be, at least in part, a matter of temperament. Weaknesses and strengths in decisional competence need to be defined in terms of a range of possibilities or decisional pathology, as follows:
- some cannot decide for themselves or for others
- some cannot decide for themselves but can for others
- some can decide for themselves but not for others
- some can decide for themselves and for others

The effective Head is able to assess his or her own position within this range of possibilities and use this evaluation as a base and reference for building up decisional competence which is suited to the needs of the school. In headship, taking a decision basically means choosing between alternatives — to do nothing or to do something. If the latter course is chosen, several alternatives will nearly always present themselves. If possible, these need to be narrowed down to two possible courses of action, from which the final choice is made. If these two final choices are regarded as genuinely equal and all efforts to establish an order of preference fail, one of the two should be arbitrarily chosen. But once it is chosen it should be adhered to.

In this process, the involvement of others in the decision, to one degree or another, is inevitable. The involvement of others is often undertaken by means of formal meetings for which good meeting management is essential. It may, however, be undertaken through informal meetings or even casual encounters with others. The scope and scale of the decision involved are the critical variables for choosing which decision making process is used. There is no need to standardise the process for all decisions. Indeed, it might be regarded as an ineffective decision to do so. An abdication of judgement would be implied, whereas the continual exercise of judgement is the mark of the effective Head over the process of decision. Some decisions need to engage the minds of everyone, some the minds of only a few, some can be unilateral. A monopoly of process at any one of these three levels is likely to prove an ineffective mechanism. It may be noted in this connection that the object of a decision made in favour of doing *something*, as opposed to doing *nothing*, is to cause a change. In a sense anyone can make and take decisions if by that is meant mental and verbal activity. But a decision taken responsibly is so because it takes into account the feasibility of what is decided and guarantees the resource commitment by which this becomes possible.

This is the main reason for involving others in decision making, particularly those who are to be affected by the decision taken. The decision involved may be aimed at changing a part or even the whole of an organisation. The commitment and effort of each individual in practice are required to make the decision effective. This is more likely to happen if the person concerned has been previously enabled to identify with the decision. If the Head chooses to make a unilateral decision, then at least there should be an occasion to explain why the particular solution has been selected. There might also be the chance, at the stage before its implementation, for other staff to suggest modifications in detail or, if only the principle of the decision has been decided by the Head, to suggest the details for its actual implementation.

Sometimes problems arise or directives arrive at the school which are precedents or for which no obvious solutions or responses suggest themselves. Such occasions present the Head with classic opportunities to find a way through by *building* a decision. By an extended process of generating values and viewpoints from many quarters, the organisation learns about itself, its needs and what it ought to be and to have. In this climate of heightened thought and discussion, the main weight of opinion becomes clearer and the right decision to take suggests itself. If it does not, at least the Head is in a better position to be able to exercise his or her own judgement on behalf of the school.

The timing of decisions is important. The majority of decisions in the primary school are a routine part of the regular process of problem solving with regard to tactical matters — the achievement of objectives already set. But from time to time, larger and more far-reaching decisions need to be taken on strategic matters — the setting of new or further objectives.

It is often said that one should never take a decision until one must. On the other hand it is also said that the one who hesitates is lost. Clearly, there is a need to time decisions well. A decision taken too early, before all the facts are known, before all the relevant people have been approached and, indeed, before the problem itself has had time to mature enough to be seen and properly understood, may be a poor decision for those reasons. In contrast — and this is the more common shortcoming — a decision can be taken too late. A matter neglected can turn into a major problem. An opportunity which should have been seized can be lost through inactivity in decision making.

As well as the timing of a decision, the state of the decision maker needs to be a matter of consideration. If those involved in the decision-making process and the eventual decision taker are under duress or in a state of fatigue, their decisions are likely to be less good than those made and taken at leisure and in a healthy frame of mind. Arranging a meeting with staff at the end of a stressful day or week, or with a fractious person after a particular upset, may not result in good decision-making; these are not the best times to choose.

Decisions are always about directions and, therefore, objectives. At times, quickness and despatch in taking decisions look good and can create confidence in others and a certain reputation for being able to act. Being decisive in this way, together with being concise, precise and incisive is doubtless a virtue and a useful characteristic of the manager. However, it can apply to some decisions but not to others. Being decisive is not good if thought of only in terms of speed and unilateral conduct: it may imply superficiality. Being decisive has a more substantial meaning than this. After the full process of decision making has been conducted among all those to be involved and the time to decide has finally come, the Head can also be decisive in taking the decision with clarity, confidence and conviction on the basis of adequate evidence and deliberation.

It may be seen from this chapter that the Head who is effective is much more than the formal leader of the school. This larger reality of leadership can be built, confirmed and improved by giving attention to the development of understanding and expertise in five areas as follows:
- leadership style
- grounds of leadership
- technical competence in leadership
- interpersonal competence in leadership
- decisional competence in leadership

Postscript on leadership

Overall, the leadership of the Head is seen exclusively in terms of achieving the unity of the school: this need not imply uniformity. With diversity there can still be unity. Indeed, such a form of unity can be even stronger than one based on uniformity. There is strength in unity and weakness in disunity. Unity involves a strong and common loyalty to the school, which means, in practice, to the people who work in it, together with a shared sense of purpose. More than ever before, the primary school needs to convey its unity to the community. Lack of unity is a recipe for increasing opposition from without.

4

Reviewing staff performance

Staff management is one of the foremost areas of responsibility of the primary school Head. Both the teaching and the non-teaching staff — together with the children — form the organisation. If they are all well organised and happy in their work, it is trite but true to say that the school is likely to be successful.

One way of thinking about this important topic, with a view to achieving the desired coherence and satisfaction of the staff, is through the concept of structure. This is the particular distribution of jobs, authority and positions or titles prevailing — that is, at any time the work that everybody should be doing and is authorised to do. What actually prevails, of course, may be far removed from what was intended. The Head may plan and design a structure but it may never become reality. He or she may subsequently spend much effort trying to obtain what was originally wanted, or trying to maintain the desired structure once it has been obtained. The impediments to be overcome are often the appearance of unexpected events, such as staff resignations, but not uncommonly impediments arise through misjudging staff and their abilities, including the way they relate to others.

It needs to be borne in mind that structure is not an end in itself. It is meant to be the means by which the objectives of the school are reached. The eye must be firmly fixed on the performance of the school when contemplating changes in the structure. Efforts which make the structure an end in itself or attempt to make it conform to a design ideal can be misdirected and futile at best, and at worst fatal.

Structure needs to be flexible. It must accommodate different personalities, interests and abilities. As time passes the structure must take account of the comings and goings of people, changes in resources other than people and the successive generations of children — but above all it must cope with changes in the task of the school.

None of these points, however, is intended to imply that structure will work by itself. There is an argument that under certain circumstances people can be left to sort themselves out, which means arriving at a structure by allowing natural forces to work and a process of attrition to occur. This can apply to schools in respect of minor sub-sections of the structure — as when two or three people volunteer to do something together and make all the necessary arrangements themselves or decide how they will structure themselves. But this cannot apply to the school as a whole. When all aspects and considerations have been taken into account, the Head has to design and implement a structure and then be prepared to modify it constantly.

If the structure is right for the school and is suitably adjusted to cater for internal and external changes, the main job is to get it working as intended. The Head needs to exercise political will to do this, since some people may default on their agreed duties for one reason or another, falling short in either the extent or the quality of the work they do. At the same time, others may try to exceed their terms of reference. This may arise simply from exuberance and enthusiasm but it can arise less innocently — though worthily — when an individual seeks excessive prominence at the expense of colleagues. On the other hand, there can be examples of more unworthy activities, inspired by malevolence towards a colleague or the Head. Disruption of the structure in such cases can be the result of psychological activity — such as active discouragement of others — as well as actually taking over another's sphere of work.

The structure as defined needs to be simple, clear and readily communicable. People have to learn the structure. Tortuous arrangements or complicated structures are a recipe for problems. Simplicity is likely to mean that few constraints are imposed formally upon individuals — that is, they have as much discretion as possible. This should leave room for creative initiative and job satisfaction. Such constraints as policy and circumstances require need to be made plain. It is the member of staff's designated place in the structure that becomes the basis for any review of his/her work.

Continuing responsibility

Given that the structure is the main instrument for achieving the desired performance of the school, it follows that the effective Head is one who gives it continuing attention. A major restructuring may be a rare event but is sometimes necessary when jobs, authority and positions have become hopelessly muddled. When the structure is basically sound and established, it needs constant fine tuning.

The rational and systematic approach used in this task consists of the following steps:

1   undertake a job analysis
2   formulate a job specification
3   write a job description
4   appoint a person to the job
5   brief the appointed person, using the job description
6   provide support and developmental opportunities
7   review performance at suitable time intervals

The effective Head becomes habituated to taking these steps in enabling staff to give of their best. A structure is good if it permits this to happen and bad if it does not. A good structure facilitates communication, shared perceptions and understandings, a high level of awareness of issues and problems in the school, and the opportunity to make creative suggestions and responses towards their clarification or solution.

In a given structure, performance may or may not be properly monitored and appraised. Achievement may or may not be noted and rewarded or acknowledged. Underachievement may be ignored or acted upon. There may or may not be plans for staff development in anticipation of expected changes in the needs of the school or to support an innovation which is in the offing.

Whether the structure is working well or not can be gauged by expressions of satisfaction or dissatisfaction by staff themselves and indirectly by comments from children or parents. Other indicators may include the absenteeism, lateness and turnover rates of staff and children, and the take-up of in-service training opportunities.

It is tempting to leave the structure alone when it is working well. Disturbing it when people are happy in their work may seem a harsh thing to do. Yet performance is not always as good as it could be and nearly always there is additional or alternative work which ought to be done. The anticipation of a future need in any case requires a disturbance of present arrangements. The Head's intervention can usually be seen to be justified in cases of palpable neglect or malperformance, though sometimes individuals are unable or unwilling to see any shortcomings in themselves. For example, a teacher confessed that she loved the primary school in which she had worked for many years — apparently to the satisfaction of all concerned. A new Head arrived and was putting pressure on her to cover a wider syllabus and to improve the use of her contact teaching time. She became terribly upset by this and as the weeks passed the Head became for her a disruptive and destabilising figure in her life, bringing her almost to the point of breakdown.

This is a disturbing but not uncommon case. Staff can settle down in a job for many years. They accommodate themselves to the job. The absence of negative feedback on their work is taken as proof that others are in favour of it. Positive feedback by way of the complimentary remarks from parents, the responses of the children and the respect of colleagues helps to build up a self-image of competence, reliability and good standing. Teaching methods are worked out to the individual teacher's own satisfaction and are regularly employed, giving security and relief from anxiety. Tested ways and means seem to meet the needs of successive generations of children. It comes as something of a shock to find one day that a Head is critical to the point of being determined to cause changes in long held views and practices. The Head is saying, in effect, that private comfort and public needs are in conflict. For the Head to do this can take great courage. The staff involved may be formidable figures. The effective Head is one who is prepared to tackle structural deficiencies but on grounds for which he or she has sufficient evidence, doing so with great humanity and firmness as required, and if possible without alienating the persons concerned. Above all, he or she actually achieves the changes desired.

Helping staff to develop

The majority of teachers are keen to improve their own teaching and their effectiveness in the jobs they have to do around and for the school in general. It may be assumed that no-one deliberately sets out to be ineffective. At a given time, probably one third are actively seeking promotion and are anxious to prove only how receptive to self-improvement they are and how effective their job performance is. Another third are probably less interested in promotion, especially if it is away from their present schools, but are no less persistent in looking for ways to sustain and improve their work. The final third may include a small number of poor or negligent teachers but mostly consists of those who, for one reason or another, have lost a strong forward thrust to take risks, to experiment, to adapt and to accommodate to new conditions and circumstances.

These three groups may correlate with age, but not necessarily so. Proneness to fatigue, loss of health, indifference to promotion and higher income, and becoming long established in their homes and their communities may affect some older teachers. Some may be resistant to changes in their settled way of life. Yet many are enterprising and experimental throughout their teaching careers and put some younger teachers to shame. With age there may be wide-ranging and valuable experience which results in strong convictions; these cannot and should not be lightly discarded by the job holder or disregarded by the Head.

All who are on the payroll are inescapably subject to some form of scrutiny of their work. For the most part this has taken place informally in primary schools. It operates when colleagues work together or make comments on or criticisms of each other's work. The Head is often active in offering praise, giving support and advice, and correction. The review of any person's performance at work is sterile if not accompanied by clear discussion and direction on how to improve. Importantly, this is likely to include learning opportunities to aid peformance improvement. Staff performance review or appraisal and staff development go hand in hand. In the past, most Heads have informally implied or made explicit the shortcomings of staff but the effective Head has simultaneously made available the necessary advice, information or developmental opportunities to facilitate the required improvement. Now, with the formalisation of staff appraisal, this crucial aspect of previous good practice can be harnessed and further developed.

Managing the staff review and development process is a very skilled operation, which points to why, in the past, it has been more patchy in practice than is currently acceptable. Thought and preparation need to go into it; where possible, in-service training opportunities for Heads might be taken up by the Head who wants to be a better manager. The central objective is to build on the positive. Everyone is good at something and has attributes which can be regarded as assets to the school. This does not, however, preclude the need to identify omissions or shortcomings which can be corrected. Occasionally, confrontation may be necessary. What *needs to be done* in this, as in all things managerial, should be distinguished from *the way in which it is done*. How something is delivered has the greatest bearing on whether the objective is reached or not and separates effective Heads from those who are ineffective.

In seeking to improve a teacher's performance through staff development, an effective Head develops a policy for the school which must inevitably be detailed within the following framework of options:

Set 1   internally provided opportunities
        externally provided opportunities

Set 2   volitional take-up of opportunities
        required take-up of opportunities

Set 3   opportunities for subject content and method update
        opportunities for management responsibilities

A number of possible combinations from this framework can be used. Numerous opportunities now exist to fulfil any particular option chosen outside the school and provided by others. Perhaps the field of provision most in need of development is the internal one. The school itself can offer a richer opportunity for staff development than it usually does. The three main tools for doing this are job rotation, action research and project management. *Job rotation* refers to the opportunity to change jobs with a colleague for a school year or other agreed period, thereby increasing the experience and competence of the individuals concerned — which otherwise would not occur. *Action research* is the simultaneous investigation of an emerging problem in the school and actually taking the necessary action which the findings suggest. *Project management* is the term used when an individual is given the responsibility for a distinct task — either a school-wide project or a project outside the school undertaken on its behalf — with the freedom to design and take a course of action subject to eventual accountability for the outcome or results achieved.

In having a staff development policy and a range of opportunities to give it expression, however, the Head needs to keep his or her eyes fixed firmly on the objective of it all. Interesting and stimulating opportunities, exciting and beneficial for the morale as they may be, have as their end product or result an increment of improvement in the actual performance of the teacher concerned. It is not uncommon for teachers to increase their knowledge of a subject or of a technique and so become even more qualified, without any real benefit in practice for the school. Heads and their staffs may well ask sometimes what staff development is for, when there appears to be little benefit from it.

It is surely not enough to know that a teacher has learnt more about basic primary school subjects or his or her existing subject specialism and methods for teaching it, or even a new subject area and new methods for teaching it. The same goes for any other area of knowledge, new insights, the acquisition of further skills and the adoption of different attitudes which may be obtained as a result of taking up staff development opportunities. All these things remain as potential only unless they become translated into action. In the same way, a teacher's routine teaching experience in post should lead to accumulated learning and wisdom, but this in turn is of no value to the school unless it is ploughed back into the teacher's own conduct and action in the school and preferably shared with others.

Behind the whole idea of staff development and the process of appraisal which goes with it, there is the assumption that as a result there will be a visible increment in the maturity and effectiveness of the teacher's professional application at work. To have a clear idea as to what this might be in practice is essential for the Head. There can be different ways of depicting it.

Figure 4.1 offers a framework for depicting a profile of a staff member's operational strengths. It can be used to indicate where there is room for improvement. It can be used to show where improvement has been achieved, either as a result of accumulating experience in the existing job or as a result of staff development exposure.

Stage 1 registers the fact that staff need ideas both for their own teaching and to contribute to the ongoing life of the school at large. Sometimes these come by way of flashes of inspiration, sometimes as the result of a slowly maturing and growing conviction. It is hard to get along without any ideas of one's own. Most teachers are full of ideas, at least for their own teaching. However, some teachers are slow in producing ideas which are of benefit to the wider life and work of the school.

Ideas come in two kinds — those which are impracticable and those which can be made to work. Many teachers have ideas which they discard immediately, or after due private consideration; but some staff seem unable to test their ideas for feasibility. Consequently, they waste their

FIGURE 4.1   Seven stages of professional development

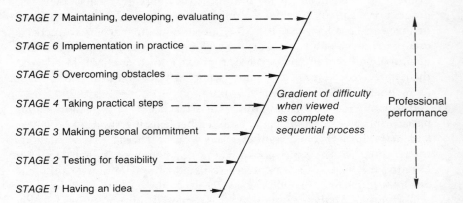

Competence and attainment levels

STAGE 7 Maintaining, developing, evaluating

STAGE 6 Implementation in practice

STAGE 5 Overcoming obstacles

STAGE 4 Taking practical steps

STAGE 3 Making personal commitment

STAGE 2 Testing for feasibility

STAGE 1 Having an idea

Gradient of difficulty when viewed as complete sequential process

Professional performance

own time and resources as well as the patience, time and resources of others before the futility of their ideas is demonstrated. So *Stage 2* is the ability to test for feasibility, sometimes doing homework on the idea by personal thought and study and sounding it out on others.

Stage 3 represents a critical leap. For an idea to become reality it must have a champion. Some staff are rich in ideas and can test them for feasibility but find themselves unable to make a personal commitment to them, or if they could do so, choose not to. Conversely, there are teachers who snap up opportunities to make their own personal commitment to ideas which are feasible but which they themselves have not originated. This can be because the owners of the ideas were unwilling to do so, or as sometimes happens, strong personalities hijack the ideas of the others.

Following on from making a personal commitment, the first practical steps must be taken. This involves making plans and preparations. Many people love to have, to test and to discuss ideas. Not so many are able and willing to take the first concrete steps to translate them into reality, as represented by *Stage 4*. This is the point which entails extra work or different work, a disturbance of one's established pattern of commitments.

Stage 5 carries the practitioner into the task of creating change. An innovation inevitably disturbs current practice — this is so by definition. Resistance may be met. The innovation may, of course, be a welcome answer to everyone's problem and anxiety but if this is not so then vested interests will present obstacles. At this stage the individual carrying out the task might buckle, falling an easy prey to criticism, hostility and lack of co-operation if weak in powers of persuasion and determination.

But if all goes well, the idea can finally be implemented at *Stage 6*. This requires hard work, vigilance and dedication. Some teachers actually like carrying through an idea to the very point of implementation, but then wilt. They are prepared to do battle with colleagues, to break the bottlenecks in resources and so to overcome all the obstacles, whether inside or outside the school. They are good at the political arts. But they may be lacking in the practical arts required to get the idea working on the ground, woven into the established life and work of the school and accommodated into its routines.

Finally, at *Stage 7*, there is the need to maintain, develop and evaluate the newly implemented idea. The excitement of innovation may be over, giving way to the requirement of patient and painstaking application. Some are given to innovation but only to the point of its being implemented, at which stage they lose interest and move on to something else. In contrast, there are those who have few ideas of their own or, if they do have them, they seem unable or unwilling to take them beyond the idea stage, but are very happy to maintain, develop and evaluate the new practice.

Abilities and high levels of competence at each of the seven stages are vitally required in every primary school. The effect of a staff development policy and appraisal scheme should be to raise the overall profile of the staffing in the school with regard to the seven competence stages. This can be done in two ways.

The model depicts stages because there is a logical and psychological sequence from having an idea to making it a reality in terms of actual change in practice. The stages are not, of course, absolutely discrete. For instance, one can be testing for feasibility in some cases while taking practical steps. But even allowing for inevitable overlapping, the seven stages do match the experience of individuals over time as they put idea into effect.

An individual is unlikely to be outstanding at every stage. He or she will be strong at some stages and not so strong at others. This fact provides the opportunity for collaborative work among staff. Some are very good at one stage, some at another. However, in every field of knowledge and practice there is a need for renewal of thought and approach, new ideas and refreshment of spirit. Changes in human knowledge universally and the varying demands made upon the school make this an imperative. So the first objective of a staff development policy and appraisal scheme is to sustain and guarantee the existing strengths of staff in the seven stages. In other words, means have to be found for preventing an existing strength declining. Obsolescence will occur if renewal is wanting.

Nevertheless, the more exciting prospect for staff development and appraisal schemes is to see to what extent the profile of any individual across the seven stages can actually be improved. That is, the task should be to help every member of staff towards being able to have relevant and feasible ideas of his or her own with respect to personal teaching and to the work of the school more widely, and to be able to carry through such ideas to final implementation and evaluation. This would involve bringing the weaker elements in a teacher's profile up to the levels of his or her stronger ones. Job rotation, action research and project management in different ways offer the opportunity to strengthen all seven. When applied to a teacher's work outside the classroom, as in project management, this analysis and approach could have the effect of increasing the managerial depth of a school. Heads often complain that staff do not or cannot take part in the wider management of the school as much as they would like or, indeed, as much as is needed. This model offers a basis for a developmental programme by which progress towards such a goal might be achieved.

It is often said that schools are littered with ideas that have foundered — innovations not properly implemented and evaluated. Heads and others bemoan the fact that it is difficult to change anything and to accomplish the changes the school really needs. This points to the possibility that the seven stages as levels of competence are found in a descending order of frequency. It is most likely that ideas will be in evidence; it is less likely that properly implemented schemes from those ideas will be found. The reason for this would seem to be either inability or reluctance to sustain interest and competence equally along all seven stages.

When 100 Heads, deputy heads and other senior staff drawn from different primary schools were asked to rank order the competence they thought they had across the stages, they revealed how difficult it was to make changes stick in practice. They were also asked to state their estimate of the competence levels of a senior colleague in the same way. There was considerable variability among the 100 staff but the trends were clear. By calculating the average ranks, the following rank orders were found:

Rank orders

| | | Rating of senior colleagues | |
Stage	Self-ratings	25 Heads	All (100)
1	1	1	1
2	2	3	2
3	3	4	3
4	4	2	4
5	5	5	7
6	6	6	5
7	7	7	6

Staff aspirations

The aspirations of staff are the greatest asset to the school. They are there to be nurtured and fulfilled. But it is not too difficult to cause them to be thwarted and blunted. Aspirations for many teachers are confined to the range and quality of their work in the classroom, at least in the first instance. Later on the aspirations may turn to promotion, successively through to headship. Aspirations to senior positions without the accomplishment of successful classroom teaching are generally regarded as unworthy.

It is in the nature of the teaching job to seek and accept responsibility. Every teacher learns to live with it and tries to cope with the duties which go with the job. The teacher's level of success in discharging these duties as part of his or her contribution to the school is very soon apparent and sooner or later becomes widely known.

Most teachers worry about their work at one stage or another but this is natural enough, especially upon taking up a new appointment or assuming different duties in the same school. This sort of worry is usually tinged with excitement. If the teacher gets on top of the job, the worry has played a constructive part and all seems worthwhile. If competence is not achieved, or if further changes are introduced by others at a time when the teacher is beginning to achieve it, worry may give way to anxiety and become a debilitating factor. At the extreme, stress may set in, with the possible consequences of endless fatigue and ill-health.

Conversely, once competence is achieved, without further change and challenge complacency and demotivation may set in with negative effects. The individual may then seek new or additional stimulation for himself or herself. But there can be as much expectation that the Head should create modifications or additions to a teacher's duties for this purpose as there is that the individual should seek it for himself or herself. By either or both methods, a continuing progression of competence can be built up to produce a performance record which can be the basis for assuming the duties of headship itself.

In all this, the effective Head is one who is able to undertake two duties — to promote job satisfaction and to mitigate stress. At the back of these duties lies the fact that all employment is a balance of rights and obligations — within the teacher, within the Head and between the two. These rights and obligations occur within the statutory law but also in natural law. For example, under statutory law the teacher cannot as of right expect job satisfaction but he or she can as of right expect to be free of deliberate attempts to induce unhappiness under the law of constructive dismissal. Within the natural law, it can be said that every person at work has a right to job satisfaction but cannot as of right invoke statutory law to compel someone else to guarantee it.

The concepts of rights and obligations indicate how responsible each party to the job contract has to be. From the Head's point of view, the operation of rights and obligations under both statutory law and natural law has to be borne in mind, together with the fact that they operate on both sides of the employer–employee relationship. The Head is in one sense a colleague to all other staff but at the same time he or she represents the employer.

The job satisfaction that teachers seek is generally held to be achieved through the intrinsic nature of the work undertaken, achievement in it, recognition for it, and advancement as a result. It is fortunate that in the primary sector the delight at seeing progress in learning and the accomplishments of children remains a very powerful reality contributing to job satisfaction for the teacher. In contrast, job dissatisfaction is held to be caused by school management policy, supervisory attitudes and styles, pay and terms of employment, and working conditions. The argument is that job satisfaction and job dissatisfaction are two different things — not the respective ends of the same continuum. So the two can be experienced simultaneously. A teacher might have high job satisfaction and low job dissatisfaction or the reverse, or high or low in both. By definition, it is unlikely that high job satisfaction and low job dissatisfaction will produce a condition of stress. Rather the reverse. But stress can result from being overloaded or being subject to severe ambiguities of responsibility or insufficient authority to do what is expected. The latter are all structural anomalies which the effective Head studiously avoids or is swift to neutralise when they occur.

The thrust behind the aspirations of many staff is their own perfectionism — an unremitting drive to deliver standards of work which they have set up for themselves. In part what is actually delivered reflects the general standards around them. Some are keen to compete and excel, others settle for getting along well enough to avoid adverse comment and criticism.

But however hardworking and independently reliable members of staff are, the work of the school must be considered as a whole and the organisation must be seen as a unity. The Head and staff, in one way or another, are constantly asking such questions as 'What is our school like?', 'How are we doing?' and 'How do we know how well we are doing?'. The last question is perhaps the most important one of all, especially in view of the fact that others outside the school are increasingly pressing for information which answers to this question can provide. The professionalism of teachers makes them want to succeed. They typically measure and monitor their own performance by comparing it with that of colleagues in the same school and with the work of teachers in other schools. With falling rolls such comparisons have acquired a new meaning and take on the appearance of competition as schools try to attract as many children as they can.

In most cases it is natural and routine for staff to have a view about the performance of their own school as a whole and its reputation or public image and to be concerned that it should be the best it can be. It is normal, too, that staff should be concerned about the part they contribute as individuals towards this.

In the past, teachers have mostly relied on the assessments of their peers from inside and outside the school, together with the explicit or implicit judgements of various interested parties — such as governors, advisers, parents, and, not least, the children themselves. Heads may or may not have played an active part in helping teachers to measure up to their own high standards as to what was needed in the school. The legislative establishment of a requirement to provide a systematic and regular review of staff performance assumes that the issues at stake are too important to leave to chance. The intermittent and haphazard attention previously given to staff performance and staff development is no longer sufficient to meet the demands being made upon schools. Appraisal in essence is reviewing what the teacher has done and what he or she is able and willing to go on to do.

All organisations have ways and means to monitor and measure the work of their members. These can range from the elementary and casual to the sophisticated and exacting. The word performance is used for the effort which has been put in by an individual and the results which have come from it. In primary schools the words records, assessment and evaluation are already widely used. All of them refer to questions of performance. Appraisal or a synonym for it is now added to the primary school lexicon.

The work of a primary school varies as to its quantity and quality. Sometimes crude and very subjective ways and means are used to monitor and measure it, and these can be sufficient for the purpose. At other times more advanced and objective ways and means need to be used. The ways and means adopted depend on the purposes to be served and the precise nature of the work being examined. The effective Head is one who makes the necessary distinctions, so that time and effort are not wasted on measuring precisely and exhaustively work which does not require such detailed examination. The two key factors which call for a constant flow of information of both a subjective and an objective nature are children and staff. The pupil profile is envisaged by the Department of Education and Science as being a more rigorous form of recording and reviewing the pupil's performance in the primary school than pupil records have previously been. Similarly, the staff performance review or appraisal scheme is intended to provide a more rigorous consideration of the teacher's performance at work.

Staff appraisal

The establishment of a complete system for the comprehensive, regular and formal review of staff performance can be accomplished without disturbance and upset in the primary school. The numbers of staff are typically small and each member is usually already well known to and in constant contact with the Head. Nevertheless, the introduction of an appraisal scheme represents a break from previous practice and tradition, so a thoughtful and careful approach is needed with regard to each of the ten elements which an appraisal scheme should have. These are as follows:

1   those subject to appraisal
2   the identity of the appraiser
3   timing the appraisal
4   choice of venue
5   purpose of appraisal
6   mode of appraisal
7   reaching conclusions
8   achieving outcomes
9   records of reviews
10   security of records

1   Those subject to appraisal

From the point of view of good management, everyone needs to be subject to performance review or appraisal. In the past a teacher's performance or track record has become subject to review on application for promotion — particularly if for a senior post and in the same local education authority area. Even for less senior posts and for jobs in other local education authorities, however, formal reference and informal telephone conversations are used. For everyone, extended application forms, letters of application and selection interviews have been vehicles of appraisal and limited means by which the teacher has received some undivided attention about his or her work and aspirations. Teachers are usually glad to expound their ideas and to explain their practice on such occasions.

The purpose of this process, however, is only to effect the transfer of a teacher from one job to another — nearly always *between* schools — and not to bring about benefit *within* a school. The principle of appraisal is to do the latter. The work of every member of the organisation is therefore subject to review, taking into account the declared objectives of the school and the work of each in relation to the work of others. In the past, performance review has been limited within a school to special status cases such as probationary teachers and teachers under disciplinary procedures who have difficulty coping with their assignments. The somewhat negative meaning and use of review or appraisal applying in the past to new or weak teachers does not apply when appraisal is the rule. Performance review does not of necessity imply underperformance or malperformance any more than overperformance or superperformance. The principle is that everybody, including the Head, is accountable for his or her contribution to the school and that from time to time this should be fully and properly reviewed.

2   The identity of the appraiser

A performance review or appraisal offers the individual an opportunity to consider his or her own work record and future needs and development. This is placed alongside the observations and impressions of at least one other person. The latter is almost always identified as the boss or superordinate to whom the individual concerned reports and is accountable for his or her work. In the primary school this is most likely to be the Head.

In theory it is possible that the deputy head could conduct the review, or even a team leader, year leader or a curriculum co-ordinator. In practice it is unlikely, however, that anyone other than the Head would be in a position to consider all aspects of a teacher's work. Above all, only the Head would be in a position to authorise and implement the developmental opportunities which should result from each review. These other staff could certainly play a part in providing information to make the review as accurate and realistic as possible, both for the teacher concerned and for the Head. Obviously, the bigger the school the more it may be necessary to involve such other staff in one way or another in the review process.

It would be to everyone's advantage if the Head were subject to appraisal too. This could be conducted by the chairman of governors, an adviser or other Heads. But the fact that it is done and is seen to be done could be a crucial factor for the successful implementation of an appraisal scheme with the staff at large.

3   Timing the appraisal

A review system of a teacher's performance needs to be established on a regular and agreed basis as part of an orderly programme — not an arbitrary one. When a system is operating properly, one criterion for the timing of a teacher's review should be the lapse of time that has been allowed since the previous review. It takes time to try out new things, to change one's direction and to demonstrate new learning and attitudes. So an agreed forward date needs to be decided on for each teacher according to what is at stake.

For example, on general grounds in the case of a probationary teacher or a new member of staff it may be necessary to hold a review at six-monthly intervals. The period could be lengthened to a year as staff become established and are seen to become more effective. In cases where a teacher needs specific guidance, support and encouragement, a review period may be less than six months in order to chart his or her progress and to build up confidence.

Well-established senior members of staff might only have a formal appraisal on a biennial basis. But the danger is that senior colleagues might be neglected by the Head, who might in fact find it difficult to face up to those who are more senior in years and service than himself or herself. Yet they, too, need the Head's attention and though they can be more resistant in attitude than younger staff, they are usually no less appreciative of the time and consideration which the Head gives them.

It is a pity if staff performance reviews are not fitted into the working day at reasonable and unstressful times. These should be when the Head and the teacher are fresh and alert. The event is a serious and top priority occasion and needs to be approached as such. It is worth setting aside prime time for what could be the teacher's most important meeting of the year in his or her professional life. This should almost certainly be not less than one hour at the best available time.

4   *Choice of venue*

There are three possible venues for holding the formal face-to-face review. These are the teacher's own territory, neutral territory and the Head's territory. The word territory is used to underline the psychological importance of the place chosen and the effect it can have on the outcome of the event. But wherever it is held, an appraisal should be free from interruptions, whether from callers in person or telephone calls.

If the Head chooses to hold the review meeting in the teacher's own classroom or other location in which the teacher works, it may create a more collegial atmosphere than would be possible in other locations. The Head thereby may be able to suggest the supportive nature of his role and the occasion. Being in familiar surroundings and with evidence of good work accomplished in sight, the teacher may be able to take comfort and feel more reassured in the event of having an attack of nerves. On the other hand, it is likely to be impossible to use places like this during the working day and be completely free from interruptions.

A neutral location in the school, such as the staff room, by definition is supposed to offer neither the Head nor the teacher any advantages in what ought to be a non-threatening and entirely wholesome professional get-together. The local teachers' centre is another such venue. But this might be impracticable for a great number of schools, especially on account of distance.

In contrast, meeting in the Head's room emphasises the authority of the Head. This may be no bad thing. It may give the meeting a greater aura than other locations but the significance of holding it in the Head's room will depend on how frequently the teacher visits that room in the normal course of business during the teaching day and whether it is regarded as an integral part of the school's daily life. The one thing the Head can do to make the best of the venue if held in his or her room is to avoid the appearance of holding an adversarial meeting. This is the feeling so often generated if the boss is seated behind a desk. There is no reason why the Head and member of staff should not be seated at ease in comfortable chairs. This could be around a coffee table — which may be used for papers and, perhaps, for a cup of tea or coffee.

5 Purpose of appraisal

The review of staff performance through an appraisal system offers the Head the chance to reassess the resources actually or potentially at the school's disposal. It offers the teacher an opportunity to reassess his or her job prospects in that particular school for the future. In effect the Head and the teacher are saying to each other 'This is the record so far. Now where do we go from here?'

The formality of the occasion of the appraisal interview is likely to be beneficial rather than the reverse. Time is set aside for the Head and teacher to give each other undivided attention. With reference to the teacher's job description, the prime focus is on the teacher's views, work to date, hopes for the future, possible developments in his or her professional practice and the means by which they may be secured. Figure 4.2 could be used by the Head to ensure that there is full cover of all these areas and that proportionate time is given to each.

FIGURE 4.2 Matrix for use by the Head in appraisal interviews

Name .... Date	Teaching commitments	Pastoral duties	Classroom administration	Management tasks
Achievements				
Concerns				
Aspirations				
Targets				
Next review date .... Steps to be taken a by Head b by teacher				

Care of the employee is the foremost concern in staff appraisal. The individualised approach to a thorough review of the teacher's work has often been denied in past practice but is now intended to be a regular part of the employment contract. This should be a supplement to and not a substitute for all the informal chats and ongoing interchanges which take place in the course of the working week.

In considering the purpose of appraisal systems, the interests of the three parties involved need to be borne in mind. The employer is the local authority — the county council or metropolitan council in the case of maintained schools, the governors in the case of voluntary or independent schools. The employer's duty is to resource the school and to secure the efficient use of those resources. The Head is the employer's agent on the spot, charged with seeing that resources are used efficiently. But the school's duty is to be effective in its work — that is, to reach the organisational mission objectives which it has set itself. Lack of efficiency can sometimes get in the way of effectiveness. The individual teacher wants to be effective but is not always as efficient in achieving effectiveness as he or she should be. To continue to be effective in changing times and to improve in efficiency are the goals normally expected of a professional; they certainly characterise the efforts of the majority of teachers in the primary school. Three perspectives are therefore present in appraisal. There is a potential among them for conflict but the task of appraisal is to bring them into harmony with one another.

An appraisal or staff performance review system is for the purpose of

efficiency — the employer's perspective
effectiveness — the school's perspective
self-development — the individual's perspective

6   *Mode of appraisal*

The mode or mechanics of performance review is an important issue to decide. Almost certainly, the mode adopted can only be put into effective use if the full co-operation of the staff has been engaged — probably through corporate deliberations and suggestions. Appraisal is a classic example of the possibility that well-intentioned and worthwhile schemes can fail or work imperfectly in practice because those who have to work them do not understand them, have no sympathy with them or do not identify with them (as highlighted in Chapter 2 on objectives). An appraisal scheme is most likely to succeed if staff have been able to create ideas which contribute to it and feel they have had a say in significant matters which affect their own lives.

Few people would deliberately set out to increase bureaucratic measures in the primary school. Most Heads, when asked about perceived changes in the recent past and expected future changes in headship, indicate increased paperwork as one of their first concerns. Paperwork, apart from the tedium, means the use of scarce time. Consequently, an appraisal scheme in the primary school needs to be simple in conception and operation.

From this — and given the large variety of schools — it may seem that the possibilities are numerous. In fact, the principles are few in number, though the precise way in which each can be expressed in practice is subject to extensive variation. Figure 4.3 shows four modes from which an individual scheme can be fashioned and adapted to the needs and preferences of a particular school.

FIGURE 4.3 Modes for conducting staff appraisal

Head's action		**Teacher's action**
Takes initiative on chance occasion	Mode 1 *Spontaneous verbal*	Accepts invitation or makes opening for it to happen
Gives verbal or written invitation notifying date, time, place and purpose. Thinks about the coming review	Mode 2 *Prepared verbal*	Agrees date and makes preparations for the review
Issues questionnaire or other documents and analyses the information	Mode 3 *Prepared written*	Completes and submits written material
Refers to teacher's file and previous review notes. Discusses with other colleagues concerned with the teacher's work	Mode 4 *Verbal and written*	Refers to own notes from previous reviews. Discusses work with colleagues

Mode 1 is the least satisfactory of all. It relies on the fortuitous opportunity to review the teacher's work created either by the Head who seizes the chance to get it done or by the teacher who is keen enough to hear the Head's views but is glad to get it over with. Either or both may have been storing up things to say to each other to give the exchange a substantial basis. Equally, one or the other may be totally unprepared for such a spontaneous verbal exchange.

In *Mode 2* some of the disadvantages of *Mode 1* are removed. The Head, working to a thought-out schedule, formally invites the teacher by word or letter to a review meeting, specifying the date, time and place together with a clear statement of purpose. The teacher then agrees the date and confirms the meeting time. Both can then prepare themselves for the meeting which consists of thoroughly prepared verbal exchanges.

Mode 3 introduces the written dimension and with it all the pros and cons of documentation in primary schools. One possibility is for the Head — with or without the staff's participation — to design a standard questionnaire. This can be as simple or as complex as a school wishes to make it. It can consist of a series of closed questions — that is, where there is no opportunity to write anything other than specific answers to specific questions — or of open questions — that is, the question or questions posed enable the respondent to say all he or she wants to say.

The teacher completes the document and returns it to the Head. In practice it is possible then for the Head to analyse the return and in extreme cases to take subsequent actions on the teacher's behalf without having had a personal discussion about the data with the teacher. But it is likely that an interview will be held on the basis of the document, which can be stored in the teacher's appraisal file.

Mode 4 combines the verbal and written dimensions. The Head refers to the teacher's file or records and his or her own notes from previous reviews and may have a few words with other colleagues concerned with the work of the teacher, all before the scheduled meeting takes place. Similarly, the teacher refers back to his or her own notes from the previous review meeting and may talk over matters with a colleague or two prior to the meeting with the Head. The idea is to have full and up-to-date accurate information and opinion as a basis for discussion. On both is laid the obligation to listen carefully as well as to speak frankly. Mutual trust and professional respect need to be maintained.

Ideally, as can be seen from Figure 4.3, a combination is most desirable, one which draws the best features from the different modes. For example, *Mode 4* might be the basis, with perhaps a modest open type questionnaire from *Mode 3*, the letter of invitation from *Mode 2* and the relaxed verbal exchanges from *Mode 1*.

7   Reaching conclusions

It is of little value simply to talk over the progress or otherwise of the teacher, however thoroughly and earnestly this is done, if the discussion — as climax of the appraisal process — is not brought to a conclusion or set of conclusions. If it remains without conclusion there may have been benefits for either the Head or the teacher or both: it could have been an opportunity to vent pent-up feelings and to express wishes about each other and the job. But there may be little substance in that for improving things in the future. It may have value as therapy but provide no basis for constructive action towards professional development.

From the performance review process — whether conducted by verbal means only, by written means only, or by a combination of both — firm conclusions need to come about the teacher's work and contribution to the life of the school, arranged in some appropriate categories. As far as possible such conclusions can and should be agreed between the Head and member of staff. If there are differences of view, the way forward is likely to be by first firming up the points of agreement before turning again to the controversial ones. The conclusions drawn can then be cast in terms of agreed statements and those where, if resolution has not been achieved after further discussion, disagreement remains. These conclusions can then be recorded and translated into targets in one form or another by both parties, making use of the matrix in Figure 4.2. They provide the basis for taking action in the future and the starting point for the next performance review.

8   Achieving outcomes

Action needs to be taken as a result of the conclusions reached. The action required is two sided. The teacher may need to take new initiatives, redress deficiencies or correct imbalances in his or her work. The Head may need to take action to provide the necessary opportunities which will enable the teacher to improve and develop. Inside the school these will be by way of job rotation, action research and project management opportunities. Outside the school they will consist of visits, exchanges and study leave. Short and long part-time courses are usually run outside the school but some may — and, perhaps, should — be school based. These all involve the Head in organisational changes, making resources available or securing openings for the teacher. They can affect the teacher's work content, authority and position but may do so only marginally.

The significant feature of the action taken is the need for positive steps in mutual understanding and agreement. In this sense, the appraisal process is a corporate procedure and has a corporate purpose. This is to bring into harmony as far as possible the personal and professional interests of the teacher, and the needs of the school as a whole, by enabling the teacher to be as effective, efficient and happy in the job as possible.

9   Records of reviews

Whilst every effort to avoid paperwork in the primary school is to be applauded, a minimum of documentation needs to be accepted if an appraisal system is to work properly, bringing constructive results for the teacher and the school. Even if a school eschews any kind of paperwork in preparation for the interview — such as a questionnaire or open-ended document — a record of that discussion, however brief, is needed. It might consist only of the conclusions reached, points remaining unresolved, the targets set and steps which are to be taken by the Head and the teacher. This would be indispensable if the scheme provided that specific objectives, with a timescale, should form part of the conclusions and action taken.

The Head needs to have a clear, albeit brief, record of the review. The teacher needs to have his or her own duplicate record. In this way an accurate reference can be made to one review on the occasion of a subsequent review, and interim work and performance levels can be reviewed in the light of it.

10   Security of records

Spoken words can be lost for ever but the written word can remain for ever. If anything is in written form, therefore, some special considerations arise. Sensitive material might be committed to paper. Facts or information which at the time of being recorded seemed justifiable, even innocuous in the light of everyone's interest may at a later date have a different importance and be capable of harmful interpretation.

This raises the question of the need for a code of ethics governing the introduction and operation of the entire system of appraisal in the school. A number of key points would need to be agreed and laid down in advance. In question form these are as follows:

1   Who owns any documents retained by the Head or staff in the school other than the teacher who is the subject of them?
2   Where can they be kept in a state of security?
3   Who can have access to them?
4   What happens to them if
    a   the Head leaves the school?
    b   the teacher leaves the school?

Postscript on reviewing staff performance

In the past, custom and practice have decreed that Heads generally adopted a hands-off policy with respect to staff performance and development. It was not deemed to be an active and substantial part of their managerial responsibilities — at least as long as staff seemed to be doing well. In future the requirement will be to move staff performance and development up the order of priorities. This will demand a sharper and more sensitive understanding of the rights and obligations of both Head and teacher while working together as colleagues in school. The introduction of a formal appraisal scheme provides an opportunity to give praise and encouragement based on a sustained interest in the work of each member of staff, where this had not been done before.

5
Caring for the children

Caring is the essence of teaching. It is the hallmark of professionalism. Whatever the ups and downs of a teacher's personal life may be, he or she will, in most cases, still exhibit a caring attitude and caring behaviour. Whatever the ups and downs of employment conditions and whatever the internal politics and tribulations of school life, the caring still comes through and triumphs over everything else.

In this regard the Head bears the biggest burden. He or she, more than anyone else, can be waylaid and distracted by the worries and events of school life to the point of endangering, if not terminating, the consistent attitude and behaviour of caring that needs to characterise the life and work of the primary school. Not caring is synonymous with being unprofessional. Scepticism there may be — and a healthy dash of it can be a real strength to the Head in facing the demands and counter-demands, claims and counter-claims which invoke his or her attention all the time — but preferably not cynicism. It is the mark of forgotten caring when, perhaps through blighted hopes and disappointment, lack of conviction and inauthenticity have taken over from a caring attitude and behaviour.

Expressions of care

Genuine caring can express itself in a variety of forms. These are all bound up with preferred ways of teaching, which can help to explain the tenacity with which some teachers hang on to their personal approach, find performance reviews threatening and are sometimes reluctant to change. When teachers are asked how they express care for children in the primary school, they tend to do so in one of four ways.

In *teacher-centred* caring the teacher feels the need to be very knowledgeable, clearsighted and able to make learning interesting by his or her own personal efforts. The following are examples of declarations of their beliefs by teachers who favour this mode.

The teacher guides children into being able to assume an adult life through the basic skills that are needed and by being inducted into the morality and customs of the society.

The teacher leads the child towards knowledge by stimulating a tremendous desire to learn.

A teacher shares his or her own knowledge with the child and is at times a disciplinarian.

The teacher enlightens the mind and encourages the child to take certain directions in life.

The teacher takes control of the class so that there are no discipline problems, has greater knowledge than the children and sees that each child gets as sound an education as is possible and necessary.

The teacher imparts knowledge in a way that provides motivation and makes learning exciting and worthwhile.

In *child-centred* caring the focus is on the maximum discretion of the child. The teacher acts in a facilitative rather than in a directive capacity, as illustrated in the following examples of this approach given by teachers.

A teacher loves and gets to know the child as an individual, working with that child as an individual and responding to individual needs.

The teacher helps a child to become more than he or she presently is, accepting the child as having unique potential and helping him or her to discover it without being manipulative or directive.

Children can and should learn by themselves but sometimes they like to be reassured in the direction they are taking.

The teacher aids children to make out in the world, especially to be happy, by giving them what they need and allowing them to choose what they want.

A teacher is primarily a resource person but also a guide and counsellor. He or she should be a good listener and cautious — observing more than doing — to preserve and develop, rather than destroy, the beautiful life of the young.

The teacher loves the children and gets to know each individual and their personal abilities and how each can relate to the rest of the class.

In *method-centred* caring the focus is on the necessary methods of learning which can be regarded as neutral to the teacher and the child — that is, dictated by the nature of the learning situation and material itself. This is easy to identify when dealing with physical materials or hardware but less so when dealing with ideas only. Teachers who believe in this approach express themselves in statements such as the following.

The teacher helps the child to learn at his or her own pace and in the way that he or she is good at — not what the teacher wants.

The material to be learned should be presented in an interesting manner to hold the attention of the children and in a way that is understandable to them.

A teacher should be mediator between the children and their education, allowing them to form their own ideas about how to do things and how to learn.

The teacher's job is to provide and organise learning materials and experiences which offer different ways of learning.

The teacher should be the guide, enabling the child to discover methods for doing things and solving problems.

The teacher is an instructor of skills, a guide in thinking processes and a counsellor for problems. *How* the child learns is most important.

In *community-centred* caring the focus is on the concern for the ability of the child to meet the demands of adulthood, citizenship and employment. This particular focus is illustrated in the following statements by teachers.

The teacher must do all he or she can do to help the children to understand themselves so that they can lead meaningful and productive lives now and in the future.

The teacher must motivate the children for life in general and interest them in learning for the benefit of the community.

The teacher needs to be well-rounded and aware of the complexities of life to give children an understanding of it and how they can fit into society in general.

The teacher helps a child to function well in society, to respect his or her country and its system.

The teacher provides the children with a good start for the future, to become upright decent citizens, concerned with what is going on.

The teacher prepares children to live within the community by giving them learning experiences which allow them to make a contribution to society.

Climate of care

In Chapter 1, school climate and the organisation, care and development of children were presented as two of the ten elements in the total management task of the school. They are brought together here to emphasise the central and dominating importance of the need for the school to be a caring place and management to be the inclusive means by which this is achieved organisationally. How the school is organised conveys the particular kind of care which is offered. The options here may range from laissez-faire and nonchalance to strict regimentation. Assuming the integrity of the Head and staff in their preferred choice of organisation —

and the consistent application of it on grounds of principle — each kind of climate may be regarded as a well-motivated and carefully thought out way of achieving the ends desired in the best interests of the children. Different kinds of climate can be effective.

Some Heads seek to create a climate which reflects the features of a machine. Everything is clean and orderly. Every part is in its proper place and works well. There is a great deal of predictability and there is much punctiliousness. Regularity, punctuality and reliability are emphasised as marks of caring. Others regard the school as an orchestra. Everyone has a part to play but can do so well or badly. If everyone is well rehearsed and prepared the result can be very pleasing and acceptable to all. Precision, competence and correct timing are the order of the day. The conductor plays the key role in bringing out the best from each member.

Another common model for climate building is the family. In the family there is a recognised pattern of authority and dependency. It meets together and shares a wide variety of experiences together. But above all there is the instinctive and dependable caring of its members for one another.

Finally, there is the less commonly found company model. The school is the workplace. The children are company members, deserving the kind of consideration that their parents expect to receive in the hands of the most enlightened management in adult working life. Everyone has rights and obligations in both statutory law and natural law. Sub-parts of the school can be highly differentiated as to the work they do and the style with which they do it but each makes a vital contribution to the whole and is recognised for doing so. Leadership and decision making are of a corporate nature. The school is always aware of its clients and maintains active relationships with a large number of outside bodies. The governors form the management board with the Head as its chief executive.

Whatever the approach to his or her job by the individual teacher and whatever the model which governs the Head's approach to the task of giving overall shape to the school, the climate of caring has to be sustained daily by countless acts by all the people concerned. The climate is sensitive and certainly can be affected by a variety of environmental conditions and circumstances. The vagaries of the weather can have their effect. So too can building deficiencies or alterations or the presence of prominent defects in materials or equipment around the school. Equally, the use of colour schemes in the decoration of the school, the display of children's work, and plants and flowers inside and outside can all have their effect on the school climate.

The key to climate, however, is the prevailing dominant way of conducting the myriads of interpersonal exchanges that take place every day. There is, in this, the question of standards — what is expected, tolerated and encouraged. In essence, climate results from self-discipline which can be observed by others as tolerance and mutual respect. Achieving a climate of care depends upon the demands which each person is prepared to make on himself or herself in relation to the demands made of others. This may be simply exemplified in the teaching situations. If one person remains quiet and listens while another is reading, the second person reciprocates the conduct when the first one is reading. This is the basic contract which makes a caring climate possible.

On this foundation a complex superstructure can be built, affecting and permeating relations between pupil and pupil, teacher and teacher, pupil and teacher, teacher and parent, non-teaching staff and pupil and teacher. To the extent that a code is established and conduct conforms to it the school will have its identity. It may not be acceptable to all but it will represent real achievement. In contrast, the chaotic conditions resulting from conflicting values and failure to establish any norms at all rupture the climate of care. This makes the working day within the school a tiring, perhaps unpleasant and even stressful experience and can produce reactions of distaste if not alarm in the visitor to the school.

The reality of care

Declarations of love and concern and high-sounding phrases about caring and sharing are meant to indicate the sincerity of the school in pursuit of its purposes. Such expressions given verbally or written in the school's brochure provide reassurance to parents and others connected with the work of the school. They are of course no substitute for the actual feeling of being cared for which a child should have in reality. In practice it may be difficult to love some children — if love is narrowly defined — and difficult to generate affection towards some parents or even some members of staff. But the caring attitude, expressing itself in conduct, must triumph over all. For a Head, this can be wearing. Disillusion is the enemy and despair the penalty for yielding to it, as this Head shows.

Having battled in state schools for nearly thirty years, I am totally convinced that adequate education is no longer possible (if it ever was) in most established schools. Many people would disagree of course. But the fact is that the popular conception of education is concerned only with the inculcation of information and enabling young people to take their places in a competitive and therefore violent society; whereas education needs to enable them to challenge accepted values and build a new society, not with old bricks or established ideologies, but by growing up creative and free. The key is love, a word you will not find in economic textbooks or political pamphlets.[3]

It is suggested that the various forces mentioned in this statement are not mutually exclusive and incompatible as claimed. The true measure of caring is obtained when the two inescapable needs and interests of a growing child are met. On the one hand the child as a human being needs to be recognised as a person — at least in the making — which involves respecting his or her feelings and wishes, discretions and choices. This stresses the individuality and rights of the child. On the other hand the child has work to do. There is production and output to be accomplished — in school as everywhere else in life. Knowledge has to be gained, skills acquired and conduct mastered. This involves standards: these may derive just as much from the child as from others but this consideration stresses community responsibility and obligations on the part of the child, since work is ultimately a social phenomenon.

These two considerations are not alternatives. Neither are they options. Neither has one of them a priority over the other. They are simultaneously and equally important. *To be able to affect the child at a high impact level with simultaneous concern for him or her as a person and concern for the work he or she does is the most valid expression of caring.* Both considerations address themselves to the child's present happiness and work and to his or her life and work as an adult citizen and employee.

Caring is the expression of concern both for the child as a person and the work he or she is doing in ways that he or she can perceive but also in ways that go beyond the child's perception

Caring in this sense is probably best conveyed in incidental and unself-conscious ways, rather than by explicit speech. In this sense caring is probably best caught rather than taught. This may be especially true in the case of very young children in the primary school, as one unwary Head found out. On meeting his class of six- and seven-year-olds for the first time, he felt obliged to make his position as a class teaching Head clear to the children:

'If you work hard and do your best to get on well with one another we shall be a happy class and you will find that you get on with me very well. On the other hand, if you do not work hard or you are naughty, you will find that I am very strict and that I can get very cross indeed.' The efficacy of this approach suddenly became a question in his mind when he caught sight of a small boy sitting directly in front of him with a tortured look on his face. Simultaneously he spotted the ever-spreading puddle which was rapidly covering the floor around the chair on which the boy was perched.

Organisation as caring

However much a teacher may care *within* himself or herself, it needs to be translated into action *outside*. In practice caring is expressed variably as a result of different levels of caring and different abilities to convey that caring to others. Competence by the Head in achieving the best organisation possible to give each child the richest and most varied experiences and a full share of the total resources available is the most sophisticated form of caring. This is caring through the professional process of organising the school. The child's cumulative experience of pupil grouping in the school is itself a substantial element in his or her education.

The first and most obvious aspect of this is matching the teacher and the teaching group. In very small schools options may be limited or non-existent. The crudest but sometimes unavoidable practice is *contingency matching*. This is a no-choice situation. Caring is at the mercy of events. A teacher and a teaching group are randomly brought together with little or no regard for any matching criteria other than chance availability. Emergency circumstances and unanticipated events usually account for such contingency matching. Both teacher and child face the task of getting along with each other on the basis of minimal credibility and suitability.

A related criterion is that of *convenience matching*. This takes place in the course of normal planning and preparation of the curriculum rather than in conditions of emergency or in the face of fortuitous events. It happens because a higher priority has been exercised in favour of a particular teaching group. A teacher already assigned to one teaching group cannot simultaneously be available for another — however suitable the latter match may have been. From the standpoint of the deprived group, convenience matching has been applied. The exigencies of the timetable or the exercise of the teacher's preference for a particular group are cases of it in practice.

Ability matching clearly applies when teachers are optimally deployed according to the knowledge and skills required for respective teaching sets. The actual ability of one teacher to teach language to first-year infants or mathematics to a very able group of top juniors — as compared with colleagues who cannot do so — is an obvious and vital criterion for ability matching purposes in group setting.

A fourth and most subtle criterion is *temperament matching*, which brings to the fore the personality characteristics of the teacher. The Head may exercise the judgement that a particular teacher as a person is most suitable for a given teaching group of known characteristics. Experience and a sensitive understanding of colleagues are needed for this criterion to work well. The temperament of both pupil and teacher in the learning process in the primary school is self-evident and of considerable importance. There is scope for greater precision in temperament matching — as when two teachers of comparable qualifications and experience are available for pupils sufficient in number to be divided into two equal teaching groups.

In considering the child's overall organisational experience, four factors may be taken into account. Each may be regarded as a major variable. Two contrasting spheres of variation for each factor may be identified and used. Thus, *the pupil* may be regarded as being either generally less able (LaP) or more able (MaP) with regard to the norms for the particular school concerned. The *learning (curriculum) material* may be regarded as either less structured in nature (LsC) or more structured (MsC) — a distinction based on the necessity or not for the material to be systematically treated in sequential and inevitable steps. *The teacher* may be regarded as being either less experienced (LeT) or more experienced (MeT) in terms of ability and temperament. Finally, the *teaching group* may be regarded as being either homogeneous in nature (HoG) or heterogeneous (HeG), in respect of pupil ability and performance.

The organisational experience which a pupil has in terms of proportions of time may be depicted in a three-stage model. (Figures 5.1, 5.2 and 5.3). The model's prospective value in the planning process is that it shows what will happen to a particular pupil. Its retrospective value in the evaluation process is that it shows what actual experience a particular pupil has had. Clearly the weightings or figures entered in each box will reflect the different values, circumstances and resources which each primary school has.

Stage 1 (Figure 5.1) presupposes that the distinction made in learning material in relation to ability levels is of educational significance and makes a useful and practical criterion.

FIGURE 5.1   Step 1 for analysing the pupil's organisational experience

Stage 1

	LsC	MsC
LaP		
MaP		

LaP = Less able pupil
MaP = More able pupil
LsC = Less structured curriculum
MsC = More structured curriculum

When proportions have been assigned in stage 1 the teacher as a factor may be added as shown in stage 2 (Figure 5.2). Finally, in stage 3 the composition of the teaching group may be considered as the fourth factor (Figure 5.3).

FIGURE 5.2   Step 2 for analysing the pupil's organisational experience

Stage 2

	LeT	MeT
LaP/LsC		
LaP/MsC		
MaP/LsC		
MaP/MsC		

LeT = Less experienced teacher
MeT = More experienced teacher

FIGURE 5.3   Step 3 for analysing the pupil's organisational experience
Stage 3

	HoG	HeG
LaP/LsC/LeT		
LaP/LsC/MeT		
LaP/MsC/LeT		
LaP/MsC/MeT		
MaP/LsC/LeT		
MaP/LsC/MeT		
MaP/MsC/LeT		
MaP/MsC/MeT		

HoG = Homogeneous grouping
HeG = Heterogeneous grouping

A profile of each pupil's overall organisational experience based on the four factors may be kept, using intervals of one year with three terms, as illustrated in Figure 5.4.

In respect of the teacher, the model is confined to the use of ability matching and temperament matching. It can be argued that contingency matching and convenience matching should also play a part. Pupils must learn to cope with an admixture of unstructured and haphazard with structured events as part of any true preparation for organisational experience in adulthood. Nevertheless, contingency matching and convenience matching are of limited desirability, if inevitable in practice, and have been excluded from the model. Conversely, temperament matching has been conjointly included with ability matching. In practice, however, it is an element which needs closer attention and more knowledgeable and discriminating use than the many demands and constraints on those who manage schools may be able to permit in practice.[4]

In caring for children through organisation, the effective Head is one who considers the many variables and puts together the best possible combination under the circumstances. He or she needs to remain open-minded, however, to the discovery of mistakes and to be willing to take up even better alternatives. Here is a Head's account of trying to do this after being appointed to a small village primary school. As a teaching Head he found it best to allocate himself to the infants. This is a record

FIGURE 5.4   Record chart of pupils' organisational experience

Pupil	Interval	LsC			MsC			LeT			MeT			HoG			HeG		
P₁	Year 1	√	√				√	√	√	√							√	√	√
	Year 2	√	√	√							√	√	√				√	√	√
	Year 3				√	√	√	√	√	√				√	√	√			
	Year 4	√	√				√				√	√	√	√	√	√			√
P₂	Year 1				√	√	√				√	√	√	√	√	√			
	Year 2	√	√	√							√	√	√				√	√	√
	Year 3	√	√				√	√	√	√				√	√				√
	Year 4		√	√	√			√	√	√				√	√	√			
P₃	Year 1				√	√	√	√	√					√	√	√			
	Year 2				√	√	√	√	√	√				√	√	√			
	Year 3				√	√	√	√	√	√				√	√	√			
	Year 4	√	√	√							√	√	√				√	√	√

of how he and a colleague tackled the job, interspersed with some reflections on educational values and principles as a guide to action.

It was decided that there would be two teaching areas — the reception class and the adjacent (presently the upper junior) room in which different kinds of activities would take place. The larger room would be for practical, noisier activities, such as play, dressing up, shopping, craftwork, practical mathematics and discovery science. In the other room, more academic activities such as library, reading, writing skills and recording of practical work would be carried out.

Each teacher would be fully responsible for his or her own class, as it was felt that young children needed the security of having one individual to identify with and a room which they could call their own. Each of us, however, agreed to be responsible for certain areas of the curriculum for the whole age range. I took the noisy room and mathematics, science and art and craft, while my colleague took language and music and the smaller quieter academic area.

The width of the age range being from four and a half to eight meant that we had to provide activities which would create the appropriate nursery atmosphere — with a home corner and dressing up activities — for the younger children and also those which would allow the older children access to much wider and more advanced aspects of the school curriculum. We decided that it would be desirable, on the one hand, to encourage these older children to take a caring interest in the younger children and to have special responsibilities within the team, while at the same time providing opportunities for them to work for part of the time with junior-aged children in other classes in the school.

One obvious concern when working in a team is the necessity of accurate monitoring and recording of children's achievements and a means by which each child's choice of activity can be directed or restricted — should this be thought necessary. At the infant stage an awareness of the development of individual skills and concepts is particularly important as it is only through this knowledge that activities appropriate to the needs of each child can be accurately provided. Thus each of us kept fairly copious records of the development — both academic and social — of our own group of children and of the acquisition of skills on the part of all the children in the curriculum areas for which we were personally responsible.

When required to work in these latter areas, individuals or groups of children were sent for by either of us to carry out tasks or to learn new skills under our direction. For much of the time, however, two different methods of direction were employed. The younger children each had a small record book — a half-size exercise book — in which my colleague would write the tasks which her children were expected to carry out. When one task, or perhaps two, was completed, the children would return to the teacher, discuss their achievements (or have them marked) and be given further assignments.

I divided my class into groups. These were based purely on age because — at the time — I felt that any other method of grouping would have smacked of streaming, a concept of selection which I feel is very inappropriate for primary aged children. Indeed, one of my first tasks on arriving at the school had been to make sure that all the children were in the correct age groups.

I believe that there is a danger of children adopting the characteristics of the group in which they are placed. Children kept back because of poor achievement can be reinforced in feelings of low self-esteem and their progress even further impeded. Able children who are promoted out of their age group can become conceited and overbearing.

In retrospect, however, I think that to group my class of infants according to age was probably unrealistic. Perhaps a more flexible approach, taking into consideration the stage each child had reached, would have been more appropriate. However, the system did seem to work quite well as it was.

The children were divided into three groups and given a colour — orange, red or purple. The orange corresponded to the youngest children and the purple to the first-year juniors in the class. There were four assignment cards for each colour and each child had to tackle these in rotation. A card was meant to be a day's activity and they were designed to avoid a particular area or piece of apparatus being overloaded at any one time.

Two typical orange cards were:
1 work on mathematics
2 write your news
3 use the logiblocks
4 read for ten minutes
5 choose

and
1   work on mathematics
2   write a story in the story corner
3   use the water tray
4   read for ten minutes
5   paint a picture
One red card was:
1   work on mathematics
2   write a story in the story corner
3   do one page of English
4   choose a painting *or* make a model from the scrap box
5   read in the reading corner for ten minutes
    bring your work to me before beginning
6   free choice of activity
And a purple card:
1   work in the mathematics corner
2   use the story corner — and write a story
3   complete this week's work in science
4   use the reading corner for ten minutes
    bring your work to me before beginning
5   work on time cards

In addition to the card-directed activities the children were of course also being given language work by my colleague and we joined together as a class group to carry out particular projects — one successful one being based on the tale of Beowulf.

I think that on the whole the team system worked quite well for us. My colleague and I were fairly compatible personalities and most of the children seemed to succeed under our joint tutelage. Looking back, I think the organisation was open to criticism on some counts. My colleague and I were rather tied to our own rooms and all the moving about was done by the children. Perhaps it would have been better if we had been more mobile, following individual children through the full spectrum of activities. Our structure did tend to compartmentalise different parts of the learning process and neither of us dealt with the total work of a child. The framework was, I suspect, too formal and not enough provision was built in for the unexpected, the immediately relevant stimulus to learning on which much creative work in primary schools is based. Despite these reservations, however, at the end of the second term we judged our partnership a success. The experience gained was later put to good use in implementing an improved programme.[5]

A case of caring

Ultimately it is the child and the parent who know if they are cared for and if the caring is effectively expressed in action. In a sense, caring sums up all that a school can do for the child and parent. Evidence consists of the growth and development of the child's conduct and work in directions which are acceptable, even if surprising to the parent.

Fears that the majority of parents want to influence or dictate mutually contradictory outcomes for their children are probably unfounded. They do not know in detail what is wanted. But they are increasingly able to recognise good outcomes when they appear. The following is a transcript of a mother's unsolicited testimony to a caring and, in her eyes, manifestly effective Head. It was occasioned by her reflections on what had happened to her daughter since transferring from the junior department of one primary school to that of another on moving house.

This Head is super — very welcoming and friendly. He invited us twice to the school, in advance of our moving, to see what was going on. He explained what they were doing, especially the mathematical work which was all new to me. He took a direct interest in my daughter and asked her if she had any questions about the school and what she was doing. When she said she had been practising the clarinet but that her parents could not afford to buy one, he there and then fetched the teacher responsible for music. This teacher brought a clarinet with him and said she could play it when she came to the school.

The Head loves the children and loves the school. He seems to aim to make the children happy and bring out their talents. He gets all the children to wear school colours but relies on the voluntary response of parents and pride in their school.

He somehow gives you confidence. He has poise and dignity but is very approachable. Parents seem to matter genuinely. It is all very reassuring. One day, owing to a misunderstanding with a friend of mine as to who should collect the children at the end of the day, my daughter was not fetched from school until five o'clock. When I got there she had wandered down the lane next to the school which we all regard as a dangerous place. I panicked. But the Head rushed off down the lane himself and found her.

From day one she has been happy and excited about going to school. She comes home and says we have done so and so today. She has particularly mentioned having had different teachers for the mathematics work, a spelling workshop, art work, science with experiments, and project work involving dressing up.

When you walk into a classroom, as we are allowed to do, and see all the work, you just can't believe your own child has done it. The school is full of work on display.

And yet there is good discipline in the school. She has become better mannered, more contented and wanting to learn since going there. She is genuinely interested in her work and taking part in after-school activities. I have particularly noticed some of the changes in her attitudes, like tolerance of other children rather than continually complaining about them as before.

This is all opposite to the previous school. There the Head kept her in the same class for two years so as not to interfere with his numbers. Then she jumped a year group and floundered badly. She was cheeky and fractious. The work was at a low ebb. The Head seemed remote. There was no spirit about the place. It is quite unbelievable that two schools can be so different.

6

Developing the curriculum

All teachers are inescapably involved in managing. They are responsible for managing classes or other kinds of teaching groups. They may be responsible for managing departments, year groups or teams, which are intermediate to the management of the school as a whole. Teaching itself is a mixture of applying variable methods of instruction and providing learning opportunities for children, which, together with leading and caring for children, all adds up to management work. At the beginning of a teaching career the focus is almost wholly on classroom management but as seniority increases it extends to include the whole school.

There is no essential discontinuity between the work of teachers with and for groups of children under instruction and the work of teachers with and for the school as a whole. The teacher's standing as a professional should embrace both teaching competence and managerial competence. The entire work of the school is directly or indirectly in the hands of the teaching staff. There is no separate cadre of people who run schools in which teachers can teach. Each teacher in the primary school needs to be aware of his or her own teaching within the context of the work being conducted by colleagues. It is also necessary to be aware of the many external expectations, guidelines, legal or quasi-legal directives and outright needs which affect teaching work.

This complex of factors is focused and expressed in the curriculum of the school. It has to be established, maintained and modified as a continuing process of management by the teaching staff. The management of the curriculum may be regarded as being almost indentical with the management of the school itself. As an institution in the community, each school exists for the education of its children. All sets of considerations and all sets of operational activities need to be regarded as subordinate to that end. But in practice a lot of work which has to be done seems to be at one remove or other from the educational process itself, as represented by the curriculum. Some examples of this are the management of ancillary staff, the parent–teacher association and the school's administrative work and external relations.

The curriculum remains, however, as the centrepiece of school life and its management as the main preoccupation of the staff, absorbing the bulk of all managerial thought and action. Everything which happens assumes differing levels of importance, being either crucial or peripheral to the central task. From this point of view the curriculum stands for the entire productive capacity of the school as an organisation, the particular way in which it is committed from time to time, and the discernible outcomes from it, whether estimated or measured by inexact or exact means, or resulting from subjective or objective considerations. The word curriculum, meaning course of study, is derived from the Latin verb *currere*, meaning to run—or even to drive, for example, a chariot—a course between two points set by others. Thus the term includes in its meaning variable modes of movement and the possibility of competition, with variations in performance, indicated by measures of time, effort and output.

From this it follows that the curriculum or course of study in any school is the working distance between a pupil's point of entry and point of departure. This distance usually corresponds to the publicly declared and legally recognised status and function of the school. In the primary sector the most common categories of school to be found are as follows:

- 5–7   infant school
- 5–8 or 5–9 first school
- 5–11   primary school
- 7–11   junior school
- 8–12   middle school

The curriculum is commonly thought of and talked about as an object with an independent life of its own, to the point of reification. This is an intellectual convenience which enables discussion to take place about the nature and content of a pupil's experience of schooling. In the end, however, the curriculum is the pupil's working day, which for the pupil is as significant as the working day of the teacher as employee or of the parent at home, in the factory or in the office.

The pupil's working day may be viewed variously as the programme of studies selected by teachers for the children, a mixture of required and optional or volitional studies, or inclusively the complete range of experiences derived from both formal study and other activities which a pupil seeks as well as receives through being at school. The latter use allows for the child's volitional experiences as well as peer group influence and the incidental learning afforded by the organisation and management of the school. Thus, in its widest sense, the curriculum may be regarded as all that goes on in the school that affects the child.

From the educational point of view this is probably the soundest way to conceive of the curriculum but some recent movement towards a narrowing of the concept has taken place. This is a view of the curriculum as the programme of work which is formally designed and implemented. It is close to the dictionary definition of curriculum as a course of study. This does not necessarily imply, however, that the children have no part in the planning of it or the chance to exercise choice in what they do (content) and how they do it (method). Of course, there can be a sharp difference between what is intended and what actually is provided and takes place. This critical gap is the prime province of management. The vicissitudes of organisational life — such as unexpected variations in resource availability, absences of teacher or child, and the perverse as well as helpful actions of other children — all combine to produce the total actual experience of the pupil at school. It may include elements which the school never intends and which could have been avoided. It may also include those over which the school has little or no control.

The shift to the narrower definition and use of the term owes much to consumer intervention by one means or another in what shall be taught and how it shall be taught. This active scrutiny replaces a long period of quiescence or even laissez-faire in which the primary school curriculum was, by comparison with today, left to its own devices. During this period an infinite variety of practice existed. At one extreme the 'traditional' Head strictly directed the content and methods to be employed. At the other extreme, the 'progressive' Head initiated various versions of freedom of choice for staff and pupils.

The notion is now well established that the knowledge and skills which children are thought to need are not a constant, but change according to the state of human knowledge and societal needs — in addition to, and perhaps because of, their own changing interests. The distinction may be made between perennial values and needs and those which can be made subject to continual change. Knowledge and skills in great part are recognised as falling into the latter category.

Consequently, the need and ability to ensure that the curriculum of the primary school is fully adapted to the present age have become standard requirements in the management of the school. The phrase 'developing the curriculum' indicates this as a continuous process. It means adjusting the curriculum in accordance with the children's interests and needs — not only as perceived by the children themselves, but also as perceived by parents and others who speak on their behalf or on behalf of the community.

Public guidelines

With the increased scrutiny of the curriculum in recent times, there exists and will continue to exist a divide between those who prefer to see the Head in charge of the curriculum in a school which has enhanced autonomy and those who wish to see the Head acting in response to external direction. This divide is likely to become more pronounced in some governing bodies as the practical effects of the Education Act 1986 take their course. The Act (Section 18) states that the governing body shall have the duty to consider

the policy of the local education authority as to the secular curriculum for the authority's schools, as expressed in the statement made by the authority (under the requirements of the Act);

what, in their opinion, should be the aims of the secular curriculum for the school; and

how (if at all) the authority's policy with regard to matters other than sex education should in their opinion be modified in relation to the school.

In addition, the governing body has the duty

. . . to consider separately . . . the question whether sex education should form part of the secular curriculum for the school; and to make, and keep up to date, a separate written statement of their policy with regard to the content and organisation of the relevant part of the curriculum; or, where they conclude that sex education should not form part of the secular curriculum, of that conclusion.

Under the Act, the duty of the Head will be to be responsible for the determination and organisation of the secular curriculum and to secure that it is followed within the school. It will surely be a mark of the effective Head in future to be sure of his or her ground with regard to the law on the duties and prerogatives of the Head, the governing body and the local education authority. Those governors with an attitude of goodwill will want to be assured that the curriculum is in agreement with the law and with legal or quasi-legal guidelines for it. Those who are hostile will try to show that it is not in such agreement. Being able to ask the right questions is the minimum which can be expected of the enlarged governing body. But it seems certain that some governors will attempt to play a more active part with regard to the curriculum. Some may go to unscrupulous lengths to intervene in its conduct and content, regarding any tactics by which this can be done as valid, including the systematic undermining of the Head's standing and authority.

A substantial body of literature has been built up by the Department of Education and Science, the Welsh Office and the Northern Ireland Council for Educational Development, and Her Majesty's Inspectorate. The numerous volumes involved represent a comprehensive review of the curriculum. They do not have legal status in the sense that a school can be faulted for breaking the law if found to be in breach of any particular in them. But they can be said to have quasi-legal status in the sense that they propound and articulate principles and provide guidelines which in practice a school cannot ignore. The following is a selection of the chief items affecting primary education.

- *Primary Education in England* (1978; HMSO)
- *The School Curriculum* (1981; HMSO)
- *Circular 6/81* (1981; DES)
- *Education 5 to 9: an Illustrative Survey of 80 First Schools in* England (1982; HMSO)
- *9–13 Middle Schools; an Illustrative Survey* (1983; HMSO)
- *Circular 8/83* (1983; DES)
- *The Organisation and Content of the 5–16 Curriculum* (1984; DES)

- *Records of Achievement: A Statement of Policy* (1984; DES)
- *The Curriculum from 5 to 16: Curriculum Matters 2* (1985; HMSO)
- *Achievement in Primary Schools*, House of Commons Select Committee, 3rd Report, Paper 40 (1986; HMSO)

These documents thoroughly explore the contemporary purpose of schooling with respect both to particular knowledge and skills and to the concepts and attitudes needed to live in and contribute to our increasingly complex and technological world. When drawing up their own educational objectives, each school is invited to bear the following in mind:

- to help pupils to develop lively, enquiring minds, the ability to question and argue rationally and to apply themselves to tasks, and physical skills;
- to help pupils to acquire knowledge and skills relevant to adult life and employment in a fast-changing world;
- to help pupils to use language and number effectively;
- to instil respect for religious and moral values, and tolerance of other races, religions, and ways of life;
- to help pupils to understand the world in which they live, and the interdependence of individuals, groups and nations;
- to help pupils to appreciate human achievements and aspirations[6]

At present, neither the government nor the local education authority claims to specify in detail what the school should teach. The Head's task in this regard is to create a forum between the staff, parents and governors, and the local community, through which the curriculum can be established and developed. The governors act in a special capacity to convey the views of the local community and in turn defend the school's efforts and justify changes made. The local education authority is charged with the responsibility to review the curriculum in schools in its area. It must make its policy known and take steps to see that each school is in line with that policy or some agreed deviation from it and is planning future developments.

The effective Head is one who is thinking ahead of present events and is not enervated by them. Future developments are his or her major responsibility. Failure on this front in the curriculum can induce stagnation and decline in the school. The curriculum and organisation need to be revivified from time to time as a deliberate act of intervention. The onus is on the Head to find mental space and clock time to give attention to this vital need and to see that it is met. Unfortunately, the Head in the following case failed to do so.

An experienced teacher and former deputy head, nearing sixty years of age and working part-time was asked 'What makes an effective Head from your point of view?' The reply was at first 'One who cares — who shows an interest in my work and offers praise and encouragement.' The reply was extended to include: 'My Head really cares. She was so supportive when my daughter had an accident.' But after a moment's further thought the reservation came: 'but she doesn't work hard enough'. On being challenged that any Head must put in a hard day's work every day, the teacher added: 'I mean, she doesn't work at where we ought to be going in the curriculum as a school . . . we seem to be endlessly living for the moment and things are gradually building up that will be difficult to correct later.'

The Head needs to grapple with both the quantitative and the qualitative aspects of the curriculum. Hard figures may be needed as well as opinion. Her Majesty's Inspectorate suggest that two important tasks should be carried out by the Head. The first is to give encouragement, to stimulate the contributions of teachers and to show that these are welcome and important. The second is to provide an appraisal of selected pieces of work from individual children or whole classes in the light of the school's overall objectives.

Management of the curriculum

Management of the curriculum of the school starts at the same point as the management of any other organisation. It consists of human behaviour with and towards others. It is what teachers actually do. Machines, systems, techniques and inanimate objects may appear to constitute management but they remain servants whose purpose and use are determined by people as managers.

The curriculum is the productive process of the school as an organisation. This finds its parallel in other organisations which are also devoted to their respective goods and services. In common with the managers in such other organisations, the Head needs to ask and answer certain quintessential questions — in this case concerning the management of the curriculum — as a basis for all the action which is taken.

- *Purpose*
  What is done?
  Why is it done?
  What *else* might be done?
  What *should* be done?

- *Place*
  Where is it done?
  Why is it done *there*?
  Where *else* might it be done?
  Where *should* it be done?

- *Sequence*
  When is it done?
  Why is it done *then*?
  When *might* it be done?
  When *should* it be done?

- *Person*
  Who does it?
  Why does *that* person do it?
  Who *else* might do it?
  Who *should* do it?

- *Means*
  How is it done?
  Why is it done *that* way?
  How *else* might it be done?
  How *should* it be done?[7]

Framework of reference

Developing the curriculum sounds as if it should be both a logical and a straightforward thing to do. But how does a Head know what needs to be changed and why? Staff and others may well be content with things as they are and see no need for change. Yet it may be necessary to change something which is working well because it happens to be the wrong thing to do. Change when it seems to be manifestly unnecessary can be very upsetting for all those involved. People often think of it as 'change for the sake of change'. If the Head is new, he or she can be charged with wanting to create an impression of being a 'new broom'. Yet the whole idea of importing new blood can be precisely to make available knowledge and experience gained elsewhere and to put these into effect for the benefit of the school. Change for its own sake can be justified sometimes to generate fresh interest and new motivation.

Tact and timing on the part of the Head — particularly if new to the post — are of the essence. Even so, with all the tact, caution and good timing in the world, the Head may still upset some people. This is the tough end of the management responsibility which can be very stressful and wearing, especially at the outset of headship. It may be exacerbated for the Head if he or she has been promoted to the headship from deputy headship in the same school and then finds it necessary to take decisive action in relation to curriculum change.

The close and cordial working relationships common in most primary schools can come under severe strain in times when change action must be taken. This can be harder to bear when the relationships are informal and friendly compared with when they are formal, frosty or hostile. It is to be hoped that good relationships can be retained when making changes but the chances are that they will not always be retained, as remarked by Pepys three centuries ago:

But every kind of creative achievement has to be paid for by its creator, and the usual price for administrative creation is loss of friends.[8]

The Head and other staff responsible for the management of the curriculum consciously or unconciously work to a model which is an intellectual device, representing all the experience, knowledge and understanding which have accrued to date. It is virtually the state of the art as the individual grasps it at any time. It certainly acts as a measure or yardstick by which the Head will observe and judge what is going on and decide what changes ought to be introduced. In this sense the model which a Head uses offers criteria of performance. According to the Head's understanding, the model which he or she uses produces the best performance. So the outcome has to be to change the practices of the school to conform to the model which he or she believes produces the best performance.

The teacher's working model for the management of the curriculum is originally derived from his or her own personal experience of schooling as a pupil. The elements of this model by default are assimilated unsystematically from a very limited source. Through initial training, subsequent employment as a teacher in schools and in-service education, the teacher's working model becomes enriched and developed. A growing awareness of wider custom and practice is likely to be the most powerful formative agent.

Each school may develop its own working model which may or may not wholly incorporate the individual models of each member of the teaching staff. It may lean towards the conventional or the unique. With lower staff turnover rates, it is to be expected that, with the passage of time and through the process of working together as a school, a collective working model will emerge which harmonises the models of individual teachers, leaving only minimum irreconcilable elements. The model by which the school as a whole works represents the policy of the school.

The development of a known, recognised and supported working model at school level provides the common framework of reference. It facilitates discussion and constitutes the point of departure for modifications both to the curriculum itself and its management. It should be complex enough to embody the healthy diversity of outlook and practice which any teaching staff will contain, but simple enough in form to be readily apprehended by and communicated to all members of the school community. Above all, it needs to be an effective tool for the management of the curriculum. A model should offer a framework of explanation for complex realities, helping its creator and/or user to obtain greater order and simplification in organisation. It should facilitate the early identification of emerging problems because it represents actualities and has meaning for whoever is using it. It should further be able to suggest what needs to be investigated and researched.

The dominant model in primary schools puts a premium on making plans and preparations in advance of actual events, to make those events conform to what is wanted. In the longer cycle of up to a year or more, plans and preparations are for the following school year or perhaps two to three years. In the shorter cycle, plans and preparations are for the implementation and maintenance of work on a termly, weekly or daily basis and at various levels of magnitude and complexity. This model is in contrast to one which allows an arbitrary choice of events and use of resources at the very point of implementation. Very little or no planning at all takes place. Planning represents a negotiated reconciliation of what ought to be done and how it should be done, with what can be done and how it will be done. The following is a list of elements which enter into this process applied to developing the curriculum. Here, they are listed in alphabetical order. In practice, the actual timing and sequence of these items as management operations for the development of the curriculum are subject to the logic of particular circumstances, fortuitous events, and the opportunism and judgement of the Head.

1   assessment of workload (pupil numbers and composition, term dates, range of studies)
2   deliberations, meetings, internal political adjudication, decisions
3   evaluation
4   fact finding, information, communication
5   feasibility studies, pilot testing
6   ideas, imagination, creativity
7   leadership, persuasion, consultation, negotiation, coercion
8   problem identifying and solving
9   resource assessment, allocation, deployment, distribution
10 training, retraining, study courses and conferences for staff.

When the school is in session the curriculum, by definition, is being implemented. The mental and practical activities of policy formulation, planning and preparation are carried into effect. The formal aspects of the curriculum — that which is intended — together with the informal aspects to which they give rise — that which happens but is not intended — become visible. They eventually fulfil or do not fulfil the intentions entertained. The elements of the management required to carry intentions through into reality have a logical structure, as follows:

1   pupil groups of determined size and composition
2   an activity or task for each to do and a timescale for it
3   a location for each — an indoor or outdoor workplace
4   supervision, instruction and/or surveillance
5   working conditions — accommodation, facilities, furnishings, fittings, heating, lighting, security and safety
6   materials and equipment
7   method of working — prescribed, advised, volitional
8   quality control system — assessment, discipline, accountability
9   renewal   system — interim   evaluation,   checks,   modification,

experimentation, innovation
10   breakdowns — coping with them by the use of reserves, improvisation, realignment, redeployment

Tests of performance

Sooner or later the curriculum in action becomes subject to scrutiny, review or evaluation. Whatever the terms used, the meaning behind the words is the same. In effect they all ask the same question: how is the curriculum in the school being managed and is it effective? The Head and staff will want to ask the question of themselves. Others from outside the school will want to ask it too, especially the local education authority and occasionally Her Majesty's Inspectorate. Under the Education Act 1986, the governors are expected to take a more formal part involving the curriculum, so they too will be asking questions.

In developing the curriculum, the Head may be predominantly a *reactive* manager. The distinguishing mark of this orientation is taking action in response to events and initiatives from others. If this is so, there is the risk of restiveness from within and scrutiny from without as the constant task of responding accumulates inconsistencies and contradictions, coupled with a neglect of volitional development.

In contrast, the Head may be predominantly a *proactive* manager. The distinguishing mark of this orientation is taking action by way of initiatives and innovations in anticipation of events and the initiatives of others. In this case a different set of risks is involved. A tireless effort is needed to gather and interpret the information needed to be abreast or ahead of the understanding of would-be critics, rivals, subordinates or superordinates who officially or unofficially make it their business to draw attention to the school's performance. The teaching staff do not always appreciate the organisational adaptability and spirit of enterprise which are needed to sustain this mode of curriculum development. Some people more easily understand reasons for change in the shape of directives from outside the school or an immediate and visible external threat as a prompt for action.

Under both orientations, reactive and proactive, the management of the curriculum may be subjected to a series of tests of performance. They are the same for each but under reactive management the tests are more likely to be applied to the school by those from outside — that is, when performance is suspect and negative implications are involved — whereas under proactive management the tests are systematically and regularly applied as part of the normal management function. Nine tests are suggested — three of content, three of organisation and three of product. In this context each test is the application of a criterion which allows a critical examination, on subjective and objective grounds, of the quality of the curriculum — using evidence to produce considered conclusions. The nine tests are as follows:

Tests of content	Tests of organisation	Tests of product
Balance	Continuity	Personal attributes
Coherence	Efficiency	Working capacity
Progression	Results	Performance rates

Tests of content

The three tests of content are balance, coherence and progression. The dominant principle is that there should be a sense of proportion, bearing in mind the child, the teacher, the school and the community. The term 'breadth' is commonly used to refer to the need for variety in subject matter and other relevant school variables in relation to desirable outcomes such as a wide outlook on life, a tolerant spirit, versatility and adaptability. The term 'core curriculum' is also commonly used to refer to required work undertaken by a particular group of children for a portion of their time, the remainder being filled with work of their own choice.

Balance

Of subject matter
The traditional labels of subjects can be misleading. Behind the labels there should be differences of type of concepts, different degrees of precision and logical structure, different tests of validity for applying to evidence, and different educational purposes and functions. Apart from the legal inclusion of religious education, a number of other subjects are now specified in one form or another.[9]

Of workplace
Children need a balanced diet of workplace experience. This can include indoors and outdoors. The degree of physical movement possible during the working day and the range of physical positions required for the work to be done need to be considered. The variety of rooms and facilities used may also be taken into account.

Of children's working/learning methods
Balance in this dimension can be gauged by a consideration of eight continua. There is a balance to be struck between the volume of written work as opposed to oral work. The child can be passive or investigative in the course of this work. There needs to be a balance between active and reflective thought. Work can be done independently or collaboratively.

Of learning sources/material

The sources of learning or stimulation and material necessary for it, need to be balanced. Too much may be teacher initiated: some needs to be initiated by the child; some may be initiated by peers. And there needs to be a balance between work and rest, partly teacher directed, partly self-directed to develop the child's constructive understanding of the relationship between the two.

Of relationships

Children need to be brought into contact with a range of other children and adults, and a balance between different teachers who display a variety of personality types. The size and composition of work groups in which children find themselves can be similarly balanced. Extra-curricular activities also offer a dimension of exposure to others. Clearly, organisational practices can be used to achieve a balance of relationships.

Coherence

Between content/pedagogy and objectives

How something is done should relate to what the outcome is intended to be. The content, the classroom organisation adopted and the teaching style should demonstrate explicitly the objectives of the curriculum. This would include the relevance and intelligibility of the content and teaching to the child if the objectives set are to be reached at all. It should be capable of engaging the child's interest and be geared to a timescale within which the objectives can be achieved.

Between learning style of pupil and the opportunity afforded

There needs to be adequate diagnosis of the child's needs, interests and propensities. This may lead to the provision of differential programmes or individual learning. The teacher's preparation for such an approach is more demanding and requires time and support. A more sophisticated overall supervision of the child's work needs to be adopted if the opportunities afforded are to be in tune with the particular learning style of each child.

Between disparate contributions

Where several teachers or others contribute to the child's curriculum while he or she is in the school, co-ordination of these different contributions is necessary. Overlap and duplication are to be avoided unless deliberately chosen. Work inspired and commissioned from different quarters needs to be synchronised. Dissonance of standards over many variables of teaching and learning, whether caused by indifference or by lack of thought, needs to be avoided.

Between intention and provision

It is important for the morale of teacher and child that intention and actual provision match one another. To this end, good briefing is always necessary. Eventualities which might deflect the chance of fulfilling the intention need to be dealt with firmly. This reflects the strength of will to complete what has been started, together with the degree of enthusiasm and commitment given to it.

Between precept and practice

The values that are declared and advocated are probably more effectively inculcated in children by practice than by precept. Coherence should exist between precept and practice as represented by teaching style, supervisory methods and techniques, staff relationships, school procedures and teacher–child relationships at large.

Progression

From one level to another

Work can be recognisably suitable for a child at successive levels of age, ability and aptitude. This should show a progression of demand. The norms employed will reflect general custom and practice in schools as well as the expectations of parents and others in the community.

From lesser to greater conceptual complexity and practical skill

Progress may be gauged as ability to build up concepts and skills upon each other. This gives the child a sense of achievement, in being able to make use of previous learning. It also gives the teacher a sense of satisfaction in seeing a return on the time, effort and expense which has been invested in the child.

From being ineffectual in some part of the work to having mastery over it

Progression involves reaching out beyond present capacities. If too much reaching out is attempted, however, discouragement may set in. There is much satisfaction to be found in getting on top of a job. The child needs the chance to master something. In striving to do this there should be rich educational gain for the child through learning to cope with his or her emotions concerning failure and success. The experience of mastery should impart knowledge and appreciation of the efficacy of method.

From less demanding to more demanding workloads

There needs to be progression as to the sheer quantity of work accomplished. This should involve the development of a stronger formal commitment to work. It implies being able to attend to several things at once and live with unfinished jobs, together with a growing ability of the child to manage his or her own time.

From relative dependence to relative independence

If education is about helping a child towards relative independence then there should be evidence that the child is shedding dependency. On the path of growth and development to adulthood, there are bound to be varying rates of progress which should be in evidence and catered for.

Tests of organisation

Organisation by definition both constrains and facilitates the behaviour of its members. Demands are made *on* individuals: demands are made *by* individuals. The volume and nature of both vary between schools. This is partly as a result of the preferred management style of the head-teacher used to obtain the kind of organisation thought to be needed and desirable. All variants require those in senior management positions to learn to live with ambiguities; to cope with the ebb and flow in the formation and decay of coalitions; to access, store, analyse and use information; to put expertise to productive work; and to encourage or require all members of the organisation to manage their time as productively as possible. The three tests of organisation which may be applied to the management of the curriculum are essentially about control. They are continuity, efficiency and results.

Continuity

Between schools

The passage of a child into, within and out of the primary sector needs to be smooth and, as far as possible, developmental. This implies that staff need to have a knowledge of the curriculum structures not only of different types of school within the primary sector but of local secondary schools as well. In addition there needs to be a thorough understanding of the technical aspects of assessment and the ability to amass and transmit accurate and usable information. Competence in liaison, negotiation and the conduct of joint meetings is highly desirable to ensure continuity between schools.

Between years

Continuity in the curriculum between year groups in the same school is a necessary and critical educational objective. The pupil grouping and timetabling policy of the school play an important part in achieving this. But continuity between years depends upon having a good record system, a good communication system and a good quality control system for the school as a whole.

Between management of class/group and management of whole school

The organisation consists of children and adults but there should not be any discontinuity because of the age gap. The Head's concern for people applies equally to both children and adults. Similarly, the Head's concern for work achievement or output applies equally to both. Everyone is subject to low or high morale and low or high job satisfaction and dissatisfaction. The climate of the school embraces all and cannot be dichotomised for children and adults.

Between the pupil's and the school's understanding of objectives

Values become expressed in objectives. Values need to be constantly reiterated. Objectives need to be made explicit and conveyed to staff and children who are to fulfil them. Participation levels are an important variable in this regard. Published documents and the level of public discussions with parents and others play a prominent part.

Efficiency

In staffing

Efficiency is a measure of the achievement of output or product of given quantity and quality at the least possible cost. The pupil–teacher ratio and actual class sizes are obvious indicators of the efficient deployment of staff. Clearly, if a class is increased in size there may be a danger of worsening the product. But there are other indicators which can be used. The ratio between work carried out within as opposed to after normal school hours can be considered. Staff absence, lateness and stress rates might also be used.

In the use of plant, facilities and equipment

The intensity of usage or amount of idle time can be measured for all physical assets. Efficiency can also be gauged by reference to the maintenance, breakage, replacement, fuel and power rates of the school. A possible further measure could be accident rates and the incidence of vandalism, theft and burglary.

In business activity

Efficiency in business is a notable factor in the public's image of the school. There needs to be promptness and accuracy in dealings with the public. Within the school, the quantities of paperwork and meetings need to be kept at the lowest levels possible and time needs to be treated with respect.

In financial expenditure

Efficiency measures may predominantly include per capita costs under a variety of headings. The ratio of expenditure on teaching and non-teaching purposes could be used, as well as the proportion of private to local education authority funding and the volume of lettings achieved by some schools. But efficiency in this regard ought not to be measured with reference only to the number of pupils put through the school. The qualitative aspects of their education on departure constitute the more important consideration.

Results

Of programme

Within the school, staff may wish to think of results in terms of the way in which they have been able to achieve their objectives. These are the school's organisational mission objectives, the educational objectives and the resource objectives.

Of performance

Results typically take the form of the quantity and quality of school work completed, attainment levels in standardised or other tests, achievements in internal and external contests, competitions, special events, community work, and the destination and subsequent achievements of children after leaving the school.

Of affiliation

It is important to achieve a sense of unity in the school. If there is a corporate identity it is because enough staff and children and parents are pleased to be in or associated with the school and support it in spirit and with action. This feeling of affiliation can be strong enough to persist in a child long after he or she has left the school.

Of public standing

A desirable result is that the school shall be in good standing. This means that the work of the school is esteemed in the eyes of parents, the local education authority, other schools, the neighbours of the school and the media.

Tests of product

The products of organisations are measurable within variable time frames. The product of educational activity consists of causing differences or a change of state in the child. Evidence for this may be gained while the child is still at school or at the point of leaving, when it is perhaps most accessible. It is difficult or impossible to isolate some differences sufficiently to be able to attribute them wholly and only to the work of a particular school and, therefore, to count them as product. Many, however, *are* so attributable. The question is not whether or not the product of schooling can be measured, so much as how many elements of it can be identified for the application of measures of any kind. From the managerial point of view as much product as possible should be identified and each element measured *in accordance with its nature*. Within the tests that may be applied to the management of the curriculum are three that focus on product in terms of the differences — of both a positive and negative nature — which occur in the pupil as a result of being at school. They are personal attributes, working capacity and performance rates.

Personal attributes

Values
It is expected that a child will add new values to those already held and may have those previously held confirmed or modified.

Attitudes
Each child should be able to express his or her attitudes but also to have them challenged and to have opportunities to explain them.

Conduct
The conduct of every child is subject to correction. It may be accepted with approval or disapproval and analysed. A child needs to have the experience of being able to defend his or her conduct and the experience of justice in action.

Knowledge
A prime result of being at school is having knowledge but of an inclusive kind, including knowledge of subjects and events and, not least, self-knowledge. There needs to be a certain amount of specialist knowledge. The chance to demonstrate knowledge is of the essence in any test of product.

Skills
As with knowledge, skills can be viewed inclusively, but with the chance to have a special skill and opportunities to demonstrate skills.

Working capacity

Variety

Children need to have variety in their work. At the same time they need to be able to concentrate and ignore would-be distractions. They need to be able to confine or focus their attention and to do so over increasingly longer periods. An added asset is to be able to tolerate interruption.

Discretion

Children probably need direction when their task requires knowledge and skills at the margin of their ability. This is the growing edge of their development. Otherwise, they need plenty of opportunity to organise their own work and to apply their own existing knowledge and skills in the solution of problems.

Clarity

Children need to be able to work at tasks with both low and high result specifications. Some have a preference for being told exactly what they have to do and how they are to do it. Others need only a lead or indication of the goal and are eager to exercise their own initiative to reach it. There is a premium on getting all children to tackle some tasks which are not specific — where there is a problem which itself lacks clarity and for which there are therefore no clear solutions at the time.

Challenge

Children vary as to their toleration of difficult tasks. Some are very easily discouraged and distracted. Others are tenacious. Weaning those who are content to stay within easy tasks can be a strong measure of product.

Wholeness

There need to be opportunities for children to have experience of completing whole tasks themselves, with and without aid. But there also need to be opportunities for each child to engage in collaborative work. This enables children to see that human activity requires the intelligent and tolerant activity of many. In the one case, satisfaction derives from completing a whole task alone; in the other, from contributing a vital part to the team.

Performance rates

Norm referencing

Where a child stands in relation to his peers requires the use of norm-referenced measures. This may be in subjective form with reference to all other members of the pupil group concerned. The objective or standardised version is based on the entire age-group in the nation or community. Norm referencing is always selective in effect and produces a rank order.

Criterion referencing

Where a child stands in relation to his or her own previous efforts requires the use of criterion referencing. This is a measure of attainment which is pre-set. A child either reaches it or does not. Thus, everyone can pass. It is an absolute standard rather than one derived from what the peer group overall can do.

Personal expectancy

Product can be tested in terms of whether or not the child has been able to have the experiences and achievements at school which fulfil his or her own hopes and ambitions.

Parental expectancy

Product can be tested in terms of whether or not the child has been able to have the experiences and achievements at school which fulfil the parent's hopes and ambitions for the child. This may apply particularly in the case of parents of children with special needs.

Peer expectancy

Product can be tested in terms of whether or not the child has been able to have the experiences and achievements at school which fulfil the expectations of peer group members or meet the norms of the group. This may apply particularly in the case of handicapped children in primary schools.

7

Managing the physical resources

The physical resources of the school include the property, facilities, equipment, materials and finance. In business terms, even the smallest primary school represents a great deal of money in capital and recurrent expenditure. If, therefore, value for money is expected, there is plenty of scope for the application of prudent financial management. Much of what has to be done in the management of the school's physical resources is laid down as obligatory procedures and non-discretionary actions by the local education authority. However, much remains that is in one degree or another discretionary. Some local education authorities have substantially increased the amount of discretion available to the primary school.

The balance between the obligatory and discretionary spheres varies between local education authorities. In some the amount of discretion is severely limited. Others are experimenting with discretionary percentages as high as 75% of all expenditure incurred in the running of the school. It seems likely that a trend has been started which will lead to more extensive local financial management in primary schools than has existed before. This means that there will be an additional dimension to the assessment of effectiveness in headship.

Buildings, facilities, furniture, equipment and materials

As pointed out in Chapter 1, the physical assets of the school are the part of the school's identity and nature which the public sees and understands first. By the same token they can convey first impressions about how effective the management of the school is. From this point of view, visitors to the school are most likely to take note of particular items regarding the building and its facilities — apart from their age, condition and appearance, which are most probably not within the discretionary management of the Head. These can be categorised in six areas, which are listed below, together with some of the critical questions which may be asked of each.

1 Curriculum
Are there contributions to the external appeal of the school from the curricular work undertaken by the children — evidence of work on

conservation, with animals, plants or the weather, artwork with solid materials, and mathematical work?

2   *Signposting*
Is it easy for people visiting the school to know where to enter and where to go to get attention? Do people know that they are in the right school? Is it plain where cars may and may not be parked in the interests of the motorist and the safety of the children?

3   *Vandalism*
Are there signs of the misuse of property either by outsiders or the school's own children — such as writing on walls or broken furniture?

4   *Untidiness*
Is the litter level, given prevailing weather conditions, acceptable and are bins or other means to combat litter in evidence?

5   *Security*
Is the perimeter intact? Have steps been taken to limit easy and unseen access to the school's grounds by those without legitimate reasons, and are they in evidence? Are locking-up systems established?

6   *Safety*
If there is external damage through accident, the decay of materials, or vandalism, have the danger spots been made forbidden territory to the children? If there are items of equipment located externally, *eg* football posts, have they been secured?

On the inside of the building the concerns represented by these six items also apply. By tradition, most primary schools make much of displaying children's work. The issue is rather over the quantity and quality of work in evidence than whether or not it is the practice of the school to display children's work at all. A school which makes little attempt to do so is at a severe disadvantage compared with those which do. The display of children's work is something of an art and a science in its own right, often being the special coordinating responsibility of one member of staff. It can be elevated to a pitch which brings pride and joy to the children themselves and the staff. It can also prove a source of pleasure to visitors to the school.

Signposting applies in the school but is often neglected. It can extend to the labelling of every room, area and facility, cupboard and shelf. Its minimal use should provide directions for visitors but may do so also for children.

Vandalism often takes place following breaking and entering. Some schools install security systems to prevent or deter intruders. At least, commonsense measures can be used to protect valuable equipment and money. Care of and respect for property on the part of the children can be in evidence in their use of equipment, materials and furniture.

Untidiness can extend into the school in the form of litter. But it is also desirable that shelves, corners, cupboards, the office, the staff room and the Head's and teachers' desks are always kept tidy. A distinction can be drawn, however, between debris arising from work in progress and left around immediately it has been completed, and the debris which results from neglect and a haphazard storage system. Untidiness itself can produce safety hazards, although normally concern about the safety of children relates to the use of potentially dangerous materials or equipment and the risks which might arise from congestion.

An important principle of resource management is that resources should not be idle or underused — as long as they are not prematurely worn out by overuse. It is important to point out the school's physical assets — its property, facilities, furniture, equipment and materials — but it is more important to show them in use. The Head is not always responsible for what the school has or does not have but he or she is certainly responsible for the level of use to which they are put.

Nothing is more likely to contribute to the image of ineffective headship than reports and impressions of unused or underused assets. Neglect can range from empty playing fields to the use of the wet area or music room for purposes other than those for which they were intended — though at times pressure on accommodation may require this. Neglect can also involve electrical or other equipment which remains unused and stored away in cupboards or dark corners. In short, the effective Head is one who gets the very best use out of limited resources rather than one who has acquired more elaborate and expensive resources but cannot command their full and productive use. In other words, effectiveness is a function of resource *employment* rather than resource *possession* in respect of the school's buildings, facilities, furniture, equipment and materials.

Remarkable results have been accomplished in the adaptive and imaginative use of space in primary schools in the last 30 years. Corridors have been incorporated for teaching purposes, for storage or for displaying children's work. Cloakrooms have been modified and corners carpeted and illuminated to increase usable floor and wall areas. Currently, the internal decorative state of primary schools is generally worse than it has been for many years. Yet many Heads refuse to accept the limitations imposed by local education authorities and manage to raise the cash and the labour to improve the internal decoration of the school themselves.

Managing the physical assets of the school, at rock bottom, is to keep the school open and operating normally. In everyday language there is the interesting adjective *resourceful* — which is commonly applied to leadership as demonstrated by effective Heads. Some Heads are all too ready to give way to the difficulties which can beset a school. In contrast, the Head in the following case was resourceful and must be judged effective.

In the middle of the bitter winter month of February, 1986, thieves broke into a Dorset village school and stole 700 litres of heating oil. The children and staff arrived at school the next day with snow falling to find the school without heating. The Head and teachers organised music and movement and other physical activities for the children, whilst parents were telephoned to bring a variety of heating appliances from their homes to the school. The result was a successful day's schooling.

In a very different case a lack of resourceful leadership by the Head seems to have existed.

In a village school early in 1986 it was found that the wooden floor of the boys' lavatory was sodden with urine. This condition had been noted and reported to the local education authority over six years previously but the floor had now reached a state of total disintegration. In the same school, among a number of other dangerous features were a towel dispenser mounted above a wall heater, a live wall socket and electric cable within inches of a urinal bowl, and rusty wall-mounted electric heaters within 'spraying distance' of the boys' urinal.

Resourceful leadership in this case could not be expected to find the relatively easy but still imaginative solution demonstrated by the Head in the case concerning the stolen oil. The Head would have to find ways and means of stirring the local education authority into action, mobilising local opinion, and perhaps mounting a locally funded repair and replacement scheme.

Business efficiency

A primary school needs to be run on sound business lines. This means achieving efficiency and effectiveness in practice in two main spheres, both of which were specifically included in Figure 1.2 in Chapter 1. These are financial management and systems management.

Financial management

Careful financial management is a duty needing to be exercised just as much in the public sector as in private sector organisations. Although the finances involved are critical for the control and work of the school, financial management has been a low priority interest among the staff of primary schools. This may not be surprising in view of the fact that most staff personally handle little money and may not be responsible for a budget of their own. But it may be surprising in view of the fact that every teacher, in effect, spends money. In doing so a Head and staff may not consider too closely the extravagant use of the telephone, the hiring of local transport at uncompetitive rates, mistakes and wrong procedures for ordering stock from their local education authority, the casual handling of private funds raised for the school and failure to use the budget internally to obtain required curricular innovations or modifications.

The raising of private funds by primary schools is now on an extensive scale in some parts of the country. Greater discretion over official funds is now in the offing for some schools. As a result, there are good reasons why financial management should form a more prominent part in thinking and practice in the primary school. To this end, every opportunity and encouragement should be given to individual teachers to have a budget of their own, however small it might be. They should be properly accountable for it. How they spend it would need to be linked to their overall performance under an appraisal scheme. Something needs to be accomplished with it whether the amount is small or large. In due course, extending the financial discretion of teachers will require internal or external training. A financial responsibility needs to be accompanied by a brief, together with clear guidelines.

A school may be a particularly happy place in which to work as a teacher. It may produce hard-working and high-achieving pupils. The staff may be devoted and productive in their work. It falls to the lot of the Head, however, to see that such outcomes are reached with as much efficiency as possible. By minimising costs wherever this is possible without a reduction in the desired outcomes, resources are made available for additional enterprises and for emergencies. This is a practical aspect of a managerial duty. But there is also a moral aspect to it. The very best and most desirable outcomes ought to be realised with minimum cost to public funds, much of which comes from those who have no direct interest in the school.

Teachers are usually unaccustomed to considering the need for economy in school. Their sensitivities are well developed in most spheres of thought and practice but business efficiency is commonly neglected and sometimes feared. Yet teachers staff schools which are costly to run. The following case illustrates the point.

Two groups of 16 deputy head teachers from the primary sector were asked to discuss in sub-groups of four how they would save a sum of £500 from their school's expenditure in the current financial year. Six of the eight sub-groups reported that the members in their respective schools could save it without too much trouble and without damage to educational outcomes by making certain specified economies in the use of consumable materials, notably paper, by the children.

Their relief at the relative ease with which they had despatched the exercise was shaken, however, on being asked why they had not already done it in reality.

The effective Head is one who cultivates efficiency. Unfortunately, the input budgeting system which dominates the public sector in general, and the local education authority's resourcing of schools in particular, seems to be incapable of rewarding efficiency. The financial autonomy of the school which some local education authorities are establishing, however, may enable schools to reward themselves for their own efficiency. In financial management, the essential principle is to give constant attention to the two sides of the equation which presupposes a balance between income and expenditure. Sources of revenue should be maintained and, if possible, increased. Spending should be minimised to obtain the quantity and quality of output required. In other words, every act of spending should be subject to cost–benefit analysis.

There are a considerable number of elements to the finances of a primary school. The effective Head will have drawn them all together into one coherent system which can then be managed. Towards this end it is helpful to represent the system diagramatically. Figure 7.1 is an example.[10]

In the maintained sector, the primary school has an official income from the local education authority. This is regarded as sufficient for the school to discharge its legal obligations. But some schools in addition generate unofficial income or private funding from the communities which they serve. Hence the two main parts to the system depicted as Figure 7.1, references to which are given as (**A**), (**B**), (**C**) etc, as follows. The official funding depends on the number of children in attendance calculated on a per-capita basis (**C**). Added to this there could be a special allowance if the school is below a certain size (**A**) or if there is deprivation (**B**). There would also be income to meet the administrative expenses of the school (**D**) and there could be some benefits from income which the local education authority derives from letting the school premises (**E**). The local authority can, and sometimes does, withhold a proportion of the school's allowance pending, for example, the settlement of the authority's own moves for economies or the resolution of salary negotiations. These five sums (**A–E**) make up the school's general allowance (**F**).

The financial practices of the many local education authorities vary. It is usual, however, for some kind of central purchasing system to be in operation. Requisitions for goods required by schools are frequently approved and processed in the authority's own offices. In this case, funds may be held by the authority. Debits are recorded against the school's account by a central accounting agency (**G**). The school needs to keep its own records of what is going on to compare with periodic statements of account put out by the authority. A parallel mechanism to this could exist for dealing with school meals and letting fees.

A residual balance forms the discretionary fund or official account directly available in the school (**I**). This can be supplemented from the unofficial account (**Q**). The money is transferred to this account from the centrally held account (**G**) on request by the Head. Into the discretionary fund account might also flow pupil-related income (**H**), such as

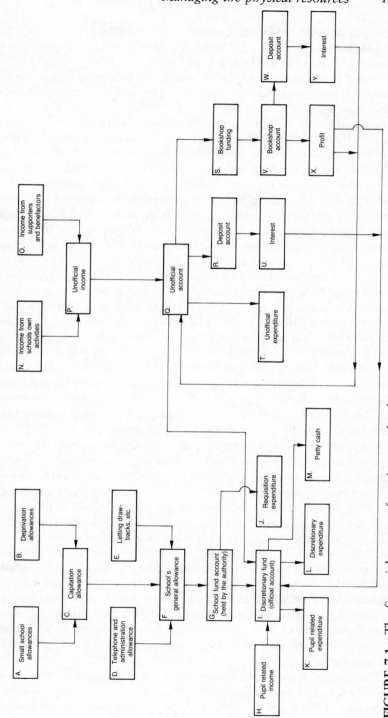

Official account

Unofficial account

A. Small school allowances

B. Deprivation allowances

C. Capitation allowance

D. Telephone and administration allowance

E. Letting draw-backs, etc.

F. School's general allowance

G. School fund account (held by the authority)

H. Pupil related income

I. Discretionary fund (official account)

J. Requisition expenditure

K. Pupil related expenditure

L. Discretionary expenditure

M. Petty cash

N. Income from schools own activities

O. Income from supporters and benefactors

P. Unofficial income

Q. Unofficial account

R. Deposit account

S. Bookshop funding

T. Unofficial expenditure

U. Interest

V. Bookshop account

W. Deposit account

X. Profit

Y. Interest

FIGURE 7.1   The financial system of a primary school

monies collected from pupils for charities, the purchase of recorder books or school outings, although some authorities open separate current accounts for these at a school's local bank.

Finally, the school's expenditure takes place by way of requisitions via the central fund (**J**), payments on behalf of pupils (**K**), its own discretionary purchases (**L**), and petty cash (**M**).

Budgetary responsibility in respect of the official side of the primary school's financial system usually centres on the need to maintain a balance between income and expenditure with regard to the flow of activities in the school whose funds pass through the account. In addition there must be efficient control of the petty cash account. Payments to the authority's central account for school meals or lettings require efficient accounting procedures without budgetary responsibility. But in the case of requisitions both budgetary and accounting responsibility lie with the school, to ensure the efficient use of available funds and the school's overall financial position.

Unofficial income (**P**) is generated either directly by the school itself or indirectly by supporters of the school or bodies sympathetic to it. The former would include income from activities such as jumble sales run by the school (**N**). The latter would include income from activities run by the parent–teacher association or receipts from a local education trust (**O**). It is probably advisable to keep such monies entirely separate from official funds. Some authorities insist that this be so. This has the practical merit of simplifying accounting procedures. The authority's audit responsibility is towards the official funds. Where authorities permit the merging of official and unofficial funds, money can be transferred to the school's discretionary fund and materials purchased direct from it.

A separate account for unofficial monies may therefore be established (**Q**). If substantial sums are involved over extended periods of time it is advisable to seek interest on some of the money (**U**) by opening a deposit account (**R**). The unofficial account may be used for unofficial expenditure (**T**). This is not subject to the authority's internal audit but authorities require—and prudence would dictate—that an independent audit is carried out annually on the unofficial account and balance sheets made available to everyone concerned.

Any specific commercial activity run by the school, such as a bookshop (**S**) funded from the unofficial account (**Q**), should have its own separate account (**V**), from which any profits (**X**) are fed back into the unofficial account (**Q**) or into the discretionary fund (official account) (**I**). Surplus sums from the bookshop account might be siphoned off to seek interest (**Y**) in its own separate deposit account (**W**) and in turn fed back into the unofficial account (**Q**).

The distribution of scarce resources involved in managing a primary school requires a keen sense of priorities. The first priority must be the provision of the essential items of consumable stock without which the school could not function — such items as stationery for children and staff, the use of the telephone and the purchase of television licences. It is reasonable to expect that between a quarter and a third of a school's official funding would be committed to this. The remainder needs to be distributed among competing elements within the school. These will each relate to the renewal of plant or equipment, the maintenance of developments already in motion or the introduction of new ones. Occasionally they may relate to non-essential improvements in the learning environment.

The following figures show how available official funds were distributed for one year in a junior school.

	£		£
General allowance	4700	Capitation	3800
		Deprivation	500
		Administration	400
	4700		4700
		Allocations in school	
		Mathematics	300
		Language	300
		Science and environmental studies	200
		Music	200
		Art/craft/needlework	100
		Physical education	100
		Resources library	500
		Computer education	200
		Renewals	500
		Administration	400
		Consumables	1200
Carried over from previous year	100	Discretionary	800
	4800		4800

Priorities within each of these subjects or other categories subsequently need to be settled by curriculum co-ordinators or other staff responsible for doing so, in conjunction with their colleagues and under the overall supervision of the deputy head or Head. The ordering of stock, the book-keeping for it and stock control might be deputed in the same way. Regular monitoring of overall expenditure together with a central accounting system for the school are necessary to facilitate the processing of orders and the payment of invoices.

The successful resolution of conflicting claims may depend in a small school on the deliberations of a staff meeting where staff decide what they will purchase in the coming months and what will have to wait until next year, or be paid for in a different way. In a large school it may be a matter of seeking bids from curriculum co-ordinators, or department heads, and then, in a staff meeting, departmental meeting, or senior management meeting, resolving differences of opinion and allocating priority. The Head may have to act as arbitrator and will almost certainly retain control over a portion of available funds for emergency or discretionary use.

In most authorities a degree of overspending is allowed against a corresponding debit on the following year's allowance. 10% of the total expenditure would be a maximum. Many schools would seek to carry over a modest balance of $2\frac{1}{2}\%$ or so but in practice this might be larger because payments on invoices made late in the financial year would show up in the following financial year's account. Estimated expenditure therefore cannot always be strictly adhered to.

Authorities usually supply a variety of forms for the paperwork concerning the financial management of the school. It can be useful to standardise the paperwork for both official and unofficial funds by using the same format for the unofficial funds as is used for the offical funds.

Systems management

In systems management the idea is to reduce as many acts or events in the life and work of the school as possible to fixed, known and routinely observed procedures. This can apply to a very wide variety of matters — from dealing with stock, broken windows, accidents, visitors, lateness of pupils and the absence of staff to the display of children's work.

The principle involved here should be well exemplified in the school office and the work of the secretary. The purpose of having a school office is that the person or persons who staff it either full- or part-time, and the room or area which serves as their exclusive or shared workplace according to the size of the school, should facilitate the work of the school. Each working day for the school office may be a whirl of activity: this is work *for* the school — it is not the work *of* the school. It needs to be distinguished from the endless transactions which are taking place in classrooms, playgrounds and staffrooms between teacher and pupil, pupil and pupil, and teacher and teacher.

Nevertheless, the office can establish and look after a large number of the total systems needed to run a primary school. The office itself should be a place of order, with its own procedures for receiving or handing out information or objects and the means for filing, storing and retrieving them. A good secretary will look after the systems established, noting their malfunctions and taking corrective action or asking for it to be taken by the appropriate person.

The arbitrary departure from a procedure should not be permitted under normal circumstances. Knowledge of a particular system and adherence to it should be cultivated by every means possible. What is expected should be reiterated by word of mouth and put in documentary form for children, staff and parents as appropriate. Such procedures can be changed and should be changed when they patently do not work well. This may be done on the basis of comments made by the users — with a deliberate effort to agree such changes by consensus.

Procedures should not be deified, however. Nothing is so discouraging to the spirit of a primary school and distracting to the staff as an organisation which is rule-driven. The system is there to serve, not to be served. Its main purpose is to establish sensible routines for as much as possible so that everyone's mental energy and time can be reserved for the creative effort of education.

Clearly, routines and rituals can be increased to an inordinate and unproductive level. In such a case, the main preoccupation of the Head would be in maintaining them and ensuring that they are observed, leaving little time for other things. Supervising the system becomes mistakenly identified with managing the school. Routines, procedures and rituals are all prescribed behaviours. They should be introduced and kept only if they produce happiness and efficiency. Demonstrably they need to be for the general good.

Dealing with accidents to children is an obvious case for a procedure: the school may develop its own internal procedure in addition to anything required by the local education authority. The state of the staffroom is not so obvious. A proper system for looking after it may be lacking. A disorderly and unattractive staffroom is not an edifying sight for visitors to the school and may have a negative effect on the school's public image and on the staff themselves.

Any system is virtually a set of rules. There is much to be said for having sufficient systems to relieve anxiety, confusion and irritation, but few enough to reserve freedom of action for individuals, consistent with the common good. Once made rules need to be maintained and enforced. If this is not done, there may be a loss of respect for rules and even the rulemaker.

From time to time the effective Head takes serious stock of the system of conventions, rituals, procedures and routines which order the life and work of the school. This may be done by taking the steps outlined below.

1 Carry out a periodic audit (*eg* annually)
    a   make lists of existing conventions, rituals, procedures and routines
    b   consult necessary people/representative opinion
    c   estimate or gather evidence on how each is working
    d   consider if each is any longer required

2 Revise the system
    a   withdraw those which are redundant or working badly
    b   consider ways to improve those that remain
    c   redesign any that need to be reintroduced
    d   inform those needing to know of the revision(s)
    e   amend existing documents or issue new ones accordingly

The computer is potentially a very useful agent for assisting with systems management. The use of the computer to carry the burdens of administration in the primary school is still in its infancy. Some attempts to do so have proved abortive. Enterprising teachers have spent time and money in pioneering the use of the computer's power in this particular field of application. They have often been deterred by the complexity of the technology but this is now becoming better understood.

In practice there is the problem of actually using any systems established and updating the computer. If the teacher cannot find time to do this, a secretary needs to be trained to do so. There is also the question of acceptability of computer-produced documents, especially statistical and financial data, by the local education authority and others.

In future years it may seem, in retrospect, that current attempts were the necessary teething stages. There is every likelihood that primary schools will make considerable use of the computer for administrative purposes in the future. There is a strong possiblity that each school will be linked direct to its local education authority. Awareness of the potential of the computer in administration as well as in the curriculum is growing, but skills for realising that potential are lacking.

Straightforward matter like details of the children and pupil groups can be computerised. A prime but more complex candidate for computerisation is the school's finances. The oncoming demands to establish pupil profiles and staff appraisal suggest a wider use of the computer. So too does the need to store syllabus details, stock letters, school journey information and other material which must be updated from time to time and reissued.

Individual enthusiasts are making progress in this field in primary schools. During 1986 one such pioneer was a deputy head who began his investigation of how to make extended use of the computer in the administrative work of the school. He made as exhaustive a list of discrete items of administration as he could and then invited secretaries in neighbouring schools to look through the list and supplement it. The list was then sub-categorised. Each sub-category was coded as being either a candidate for early or later inclusion in the developmental programme he envisaged. He also coded each item according to the kind of computer treatment that seemed most appropriate for it. The school then committed itself to a rolling programme which would eventually include all the administration. It was expected to take several years. Figure 7.2 shows the list of items arranged in sub-categories with the proposed computer treatment.[11]

FIGURE 7.2 Analysis of administrative material for computer development programme

Primary school databank

Type 1 Information: Word Processor

Agendas, minutes, reports: governors; PTA
Letter: parents; other organisations; local education authority
Material to parents
Newsletters
Notice board material
Notices of events
References
School brochure material
Staff handbook material

Type 2 Information: Data Base

Admissions and discharges form
Admissions and discharges register
DES form 7
Children's personal details/medical records
Inventory of resources
Non-teaching staff details
Repairs
School roll and distribution form
Staff and class organisation form
Supply teachers
Teaching staff details
Transfers to secondary school form

Type 3 Information: Spread Sheet

Dining-room assistants' timesheet
Discretionary allowances to staff
Financial projects (eg bookshop)
Meals balance form
Official allowances (capitation)
School fund
School meals
School meals statistical return
Other funds (eg school journeys)

Type 4 Information: Times Network (electronic mail)

Communication systems between schools and, in some areas, between the LEA and schools.

FIGURE 7.2 (*Continued*)

Type 5 Information: News Sheet

Publicity material

Items not yet incorporated in the computer system

Children's academic records
Children's records of achievement (pupil profiles)
Dining-room assistants' details
Dinner registers
Free meals
Head's diary/appointments
PTA activities
Requisitions
School calendar
School uniform details
Some other funds (eg PTA draw tickets; disco tickets)
Staff appraisal records
Stocktaking

8

Making the most of time

The importance of time management is enshrined in our culture by way of a large variety of sayings, many of which are of great antiquity. 'Procrastination is the thief of time' offers a warning to the sluggard, whilst 'ask a busy person if you want something done' points to the possibility of the almost endless use to which time can be put if managed with skill and prudence. The need to anticipate the development of problems is indicated in 'a stitch in time saves nine'. Seemingly contradictory advice is offered in 'he who hesitates is lost' and 'look before you leap'. 'Time heals' can be the solution for problems in many a human relationship.

The pressure of modern day transactions is brought to our attention in the saying 'time is money' with reference to the constant need for efficiency and 'stop before you have to' with reference to the more sinister need to consider the effects of stress and the personal health of people at work in contemporary organisations.

When faced with numerous actual burdens at work or more possibly the psychological enormity of what waits to be done, no better wisdom is available than that contained in the saying 'the way to eat an elephant is one bite at a time'. When all is done that can be done there is cause for rest and self-congratulation. No-one can do more than a day's work at a time. But there should be no room for complacency. There is almost always room for the improvement in the use of one's time. Steady progress in achieving such improvements is very much the hallmark of the effective Head.

Cause for concern

Educationally, the use of time needs to be given top consideration for two reasons. In the first place, children need to be encouraged to make an effort to work steadily and fully during their time in school. They need to observe the timekeeping rules and practices which the school imposes as part of its organisation to create an orderly and productive environment. In the second place, time management is a matter of fundamental and life-long importance for the children in their own lives with respect to their employment careers and family life. The primary school has much to gain from giving attention to time management, not only for the sake of the impact this can have on its own immediate tasks and responsibilities, but also in terms of its obligation towards attitudes and conduct in society at large.

The working day in primary schools is commonly felt and observed to be busy, frequently fraught and occasionally frantic. While the majority of Heads try to undertake some teaching every week, Heads of small schools and deputy heads usually try to combine managerial work with a full or nearly full class teaching load. On the one hand, the dilemmas which spring from doing this are often frustrating and tiring. On the other, the combination serves as a challenge and a way of demonstrating one's calibre. If the two parts of the job — managing and teaching — are regarded as a single whole — albeit in awkward proportions — there is scope for ingenuity in the use of time as well as sheer energy, leading to exceptional achievement for those who can learn how to cope with the two together.

A key factor is the use made of time. Everyone must work within time constraints. Time is the common resource, and everyone has the same amount of time. It is nonetheless a precious resource. Some Heads treat it well, others badly. Most complain that they never have enough time. But in fact 'I didn't have time' is strictly speaking always inaccurate as an excuse for failure to discharge a duty or promise. Everyone has the same opportunity to meet every commitment or not, the individual simply chooses to use time or allow it to be used for different priorities.

One of the most detrimental results of badly managed time is that the individual concerned is unable to find time to learn how he or she is using it. The use of time easily becomes unbalanced. Some activities assume far greater a proportion of attention than they warrant, others too little. The individual is vaguely conscious that time is being inappropriately allocated in relation to an ill-defined set of priorities. Drift in the management of time is often the effect of strong commitment, hard work and absorption in the job.

In essence, the effective management of time is a matter of balancing demands and resources. The demands may be voluntarily incurred and therefore, in theory, adjustable. They may, however, be imposed and difficult to avoid. The resources are a person's capacity for work, consisting of such variables as health, physical strength, motivation and personality — which includes the individual's levels of arousal, inhibition, stimulation seeking, imagery and distractability.

The underlying anxiety about the use of time for headteachers arises from an awareness of incongruence between what they *ought* to be doing and what they *are* doing. The anxiety is heightened by the realisation that no-one but the individual himself or herself is the best judge of what ought to be done in preference to what is being done. It is not diminished by the further realisation that in the long term the judgement of others on the Head's performance in office depends upon the Head's own judgement as to what ought to be done.

Actual use of time

Any attempt to improve the management of time must begin with accurate knowledge of how time is actually being spent at present. This is no less so for teachers than those in industry and commerce. Much attention has been given in recent years to the observation and analysis of how managers spend their time. This has made possible the classification of work and the establishment of a typology of jobs, leading to the identification and characterisation of differences even within the same occupational category.

It is possible for the Head to monitor and analyse his or her own use of time. The simplest device for doing this is to take a sheet of A4 paper for each day of the week with time slots down the left-hand side and types of work along the top, as illustrated in Figure 8.1. Totals can be taken at the end of the week to give a reasonably accurate set of percentages for the overall use of time.

This exercise can be repeated at intervals during the school year to allow for seasonal variations in types of work. Clearly, the time intervals used can be made shorter or longer and the types of work can be adjusted in number and kind to suit individual circumstances and interests. For example, time spent making use of secretarial help or touring the school might be specified. The results can be used to see the proportion of time each item is commanding and the likely places where time savings can be made.

A comparative study of the use of time by primary school Heads and industrial managers found that they were all involved in similar kinds of activity, but that the amount of time and the degree of interaction with others to complete these activities varied. Similar percentages of time were spent by the two groups on planning, investigating, coordinating and evaluating. Heads spent more time in supervising, representing their organisations to outside bodies, and following activities for personal growth. Industrial managers spent more time than the Heads on staffing, negotiating, and miscellaneous items such as welfare, discipline, social engagements and business travelling. Heads and industrial managers spent about the same amount of time interacting with their own staff, but individual managers spent twice as much time interacting with other managers as peers than Heads. Heads spent a quarter of their entire time interacting with their clients — pupils and parents — whereas industrial managers spent only just over 3% with theirs.

Both Heads and industrial managers spent half their time working in their own offices but managers spent a further quarter of their time working in other offices; this was almost an unknown experience for the Heads. Time spent in cars, working away from home and working at home was similar for both groups. Heads and industrial managers spent equal amounts of time talking and in meetings (59%). Heads wrote a little more than the industrial managers and listened twice as much but

FIGURE 8.1 Head's use of time analysis sheet

Date ....   TYPES OF WORK   Sheet No ....

	Deskwork		Telephone		Out of school		Talking with				Teaching		Notes
	Administrative	Educational	In	Out	For school	For others	Pupils	Staff	Parents	Others	Cover	Scheduled	
0815–0830	15												
0830–0845	5		2	3				5					
0845–0900	5	5						5					
0900–0915												*15	*Assembly
0915–0930							5					*10	*Assembly
0930–0945											15		
0945–1000											15		
etc													
WEEKLY TOTALS													
% of week													

at a low percentage level. Managers, on the other hand, read a little more than the Heads but at a low percentage level.[12]

A study conducted over a period of three years focused on the working day of a group of Heads of primary schools. Large and small, inner-city and outer-city schools were represented. Work study techniques were used to record what the Heads did minute by minute, to whom they talked, the subject of the discussion, who initiated the contact, where the exchanges took place and their duration. Their observations indicated how busy, unpredictable and fragmented the Head's working day was, a good portion of the day's work taking place out and about in the school away from the Head's office. The rapid and random sequence of undifferentiated events which characteristically made up the working day was found to be antithetic to reflection and ordered, thoughtful decision making. Classroom observation and the supervision of teachers was not found to be the central focus of headship. In terms of the allocation of working time, the Head's work was directed towards monitoring what was going on in the school, including receiving information and checking on activities; representing the school to outside bodies; serving as leader of the staff, including the dissemination of information, giving instructions, praise and reproof, and socialising with the staff; and acting as resource allocator and disturbance handler, involving staff and pupil deployment and work programmes and unexpected breakdowns, crises or injuries.[13]

A recent study was concerned with the nature of the work of Heads and deputy heads of primary schools. It tried to establish the kind and frequency of contacts they had with others, on whose initiative tasks were performed, the tasks they undertook together and those they did separately. The prime purpose of the study was to convey to deputy heads the work expected of them as Heads of schools by the more realistic methods of time management analysis rather than by impression and anecdote. The argument advanced was that the training of deputy heads for headship may only have substance if it is known what work the Head of school actually does and how he or she allocates working time.

Two Heads over a nine-day period together performed a total of 759 tasks, excluding teaching. Of this total, 602 were tasks that lasted up to ten minutes before interruption, 119 lasted between 11 and 20 minutes before interruption, and 38 lasted more than 20 minutes before interruption. The contrast between the two Heads, however, was marked. For the three time slots respectively, one Head (of an infant school) recorded 541, 71 and 24 uninterrupted tasks as compared with the other Head (of a primary school) who recorded corresponding figures of 61, 48 and 14. The nature of the work, the age-range of the children, the size of the school and the ability and opportunity to delegate clearly create such differences. One Head recorded 31 consecutive activities of up to ten minutes' duration between 08.25 and 10.25 on one particular day. On other days during the experimental period concerned, the same Head recorded corresponding runs of 26, 19, 18, 16, 13 and 11 consecutive activities.

Among other findings was the fact that a small group of Heads and deputies recorded an average of six tasks during the lunch break and five tasks before school started. Nearly half of all contacts between Heads and deputy heads occurred during class time. A third of all contacts between deputy heads and other teachers initiated by the latter occurred during class time. Deputy heads in general felt that they had insufficient time to teach as well as being deputy head.

These findings convey an impression of a fragmented and distracting working day. To the extent that the prevailing pattern is objectionable, those who suffer, as well as those who create it, need to review their management of time. Instant access and instant satisfaction seem to predominate over concentration, completion and equilibrium.[14]

One of the most recently reported studies of primary school Heads' use of time was particularly concerned to chart the differences which occurred between the intended use of time and the actual use of time. The number of such differences for each Head in the study ranged between 11 and 70 per week, with an average of 40 — that is, eight per day. The figure was lower in smaller schools where the Head was teaching and could not be interrupted. The average actual uses of time by the Heads in the study were as follows.

Work category	% of working week used
1 contacts with pupils	31
2 contacts with staff	12
3 contacts with others	12
4 administration	19
5 preparation and INSET	21
6 other, including travelling to school	5
	100

(figures corrected to nearest whole percentage point)

Heads of small schools spent more time with pupils and had less time for staff. They arrived in school earlier than Heads of larger schools to deal with jobs for which no time was available during the day. Heads of both small and large schools spent about the same percentage of time in contact with people other than pupils and staff; time spent in this way was about twice the intended amount. The intended and actual uses of time varied by up to five percentage points either way in the case of each of the other five work categories. Categories 1, 2 and 6 claimed more time, categories 4 and 5 less.[15]

Responses to worries over time

All schools use time and in the end are judged by how they have spent it. The Head's part in the management of time in the school is a key one. He or she must not only face the pressing problems over the use of his or her own time but exercise some kind of responsibility to see that other people in the school make the best use of their time as well.

Time as a resource is constantly wasting. It cannot be aggregated. In contrast, work to be done readily accumulates. Problems not solved can easily become worse with the passage of time. Duties not discharged simply wait for attention. Consequently, many Heads feel that they manage their time badly all the time or some of the time. Time is constant but the ability of individuals to make use of it varies a great deal. This can be seen in the way individuals differ in their ability to schedule their activities, the speed at which they work, the volume of work accomplished and the thoroughness or standards of the work accomplished.

Heads may take one or more of a number of possible remedial actions or defensive steps when they become concerned about their use of time. Ineffective Heads are those who look for a scapegoat and often find it in allegedly having insufficient time. But even effective Heads, who almost certainly *are* effective in part because of good time management, may wish to reconsider their use of time. As claims upon them and pressures mount, they may have to begin to count the cost of maintaining all their commitments. When time becomes a concern in this way, people usually resort to one or more of the following solutions.

1   Work harder

Working harder to most people means working longer. A Head who decides to work harder takes more hours out of the day before and after school, at the week-end and in half-term and the longer vacation periods. Doing this squeezes the time available for private life with the family, in the garden, with friends, for family business matters, for hobbies and for holidays. There is surely no harm in working harder in this sense — up to a point. Work can be enjoyable, particularly at more leisured moments. Work done off-site creates a feeling of confidence in being well prepared for the next day, the next week or the new term at school. But squeezing the time available for private life can cause family problems and lack of opportunities for personal refreshment and renewal. Working harder to the point that this happens becomes counter-productive.

2   Work more quickly

This means putting more energy into doing things so that everything is speeded up. It calls for more continuous concentration and a refusal to be distracted or interrupted. The total hours of work remain the same, whilst spare time is created to do outstanding or extra jobs. This option is most readily open to those who are temperamentally casual, easy going or just plain slow. It may not be open to those who are already given to quickness of action. In both cases working more quickly may put pressure on the temperament, producing fatigue and stress as surely as working inordinately long hours. But marginal gains by working more quickly seem open to most people.

3   Work selectively

Working selectively is stringently regulating what one personally decides to undertake. In this case jobs not selected remain undone or have to be done by someone else. A principle should govern what is and what is not selected. The one commonly used is availability — which means that I have time or I do not have time. This principle applies most clearly in a group where there is complete interchangeability of jobs. In the primary school, collegial relationships among the staff and a strong team spirit can prevail. Many jobs can be done by anyone who happens to be available. But the management of a primary school cannot consist entirely of completely interchangeable jobs. The principle of relative indispensability or least available expertise needs to apply. The Head's thinking is governed by the need to take jobs first which only he or she can do *because of being the Head*. This is the Head's irreducible workload and includes keeping an overview of the school and planning for its development. This can be so readily neglected in favour of the many immediate tasks. When this work is done or is being accommodated — and only then — should jobs be undertaken which other staff could do.

4   Work efficiently

Working efficiently means choosing the best sequence for doing a range of jobs as far as that is possible. It involves deciding the priority of each so that the amount of time given to each is proportionate to its priority. The difference this can make is the difference between saying 'I am doing this job and I do not know how long it will take' and 'I have 20 minutes to do what I can with this job'.

Priorities, sequences and times are the principles at work in *critical path analysis* which is used to control any large and complicated undertaking, such as the construction of a building. As in making a cup of tea, it is possible to do things in the order which takes most time by choosing the jobs in arbitrary sequence, or it is possible to do them in an order which uses least time by taking prior thought. If the water is put on to boil, other jobs can be done while this is taking place.

The idea is not to respond to jobs one by one as they occur. Where possible they should be collected and scheduled, including jobs which are not yet manifest but which are anticipated. This could mean, for example, saving up several phone calls to make at the same time rather than as the need for each arises; or accumulating several items of business which concern the same person and then dealing with them at the same time. Efficient working of this kind could particularly apply to people with whom it is hard to make contact.

5   Work differentially

This means adopting different standards of work output across the range of jobs to be done. There are some things which have to be done to a high standard of performance. There are many which do not. Many

Heads seem to be temperamentally incapable of doing anything less than well, but some jobs need only to be done adequately. Choosing which is which may be an art in itself. Experience can soon teach it. But it is more a matter of the Head's having a feel for the identity of jobs which have high impact value on those who will judge the school to be effective or not.

The idea is that less time is used if a job is performed at a lower standard of product excellence than at a high standard. A working note to a colleague may leave everything to be desired in terms of presentation. A summary of a job performance review if made in writing to the same colleague, however, should leave nothing to be desired with regard to product standards. The issue is very clear over written materials, but can apply to all kinds of activities in the quest to make the best use of time.

The primary Head's own timesavers

A large group of primary Heads conducted an audit of their experience in the use of timesaving devices. The result of their discussion and analysis was that timesaving fell into three categories of concern. There were the ideas that had been translated into practice and found to be successful. There were ideas that were well regarded and looked promising but had not yet been tried. And there were the bad practices which needed to be eradicated. The items in each of these categories were finally listed as follows.

1   *Time savers in use*
    - making an actual list of priorities for jobs or undertakings which have to be done
    - delegating jobs to others, reserving only jobs that others cannot do
    - ensuring that a communication actually reaches the person intended in a form that he or she can understand and will not forget
    - having an efficient office system for collecting, storing, retrieving and disseminating information
    - controlling interruptions

2   *Time savers not yet in use*
    - using computerised administration
    - installing an Ansaphone
    - having a personal filing system
    - using check lists on a round the year basis
    - employing dictation skills
    - establishing more efficient reprographics system
    - taking regular 'isolation' periods

3   *Time wasters to be eradicated*
    - being too fastidious over the paperwork
    - giving in to too much socialising during the working day
    - being indecisive

- straying from being single-minded
- failing to be ruthless when needs demand
- attending to minor repairs

Styles of time management

People are habituated to different attitudes to time. Among Heads of primary schools different attitudes to time may be found, and these may differ most at the time of assuming headship. Experience in post heightens the awareness of the importance of time as never before. Some may later want to use their time more productively and are motivated to do so but may not know how to do it.

Appearances can be deceptive. Some Heads appear to be wasting time or making little of it, others convey the impression that they have so much to do and seem to be well on the way to doing it. It is probably always necessary to look at the track record of a Head or what the school is actually producing overall as a proper indicator of the Head's management of time. It is unlikely that an effective Head is confined to a constant attitude and limited ability in time management.

In practice it is possible to discern four main sets of differences in attitudes and abilities in time management. These may be thought of as styles of time management.

The *hyperactive* Head is mentally and physically never still. He or she is into everything which is going on. No matter, whether great or small, escapes his or her notice and everything receives instant attention. The pace of work adopted may seem threatening to others and indeed can finally alienate them.

The *proactive* Head is thinking and acting ahead of necessities and required action by anticipating events, identifying latent problems and preparing for them. He or she always seems to be one up on everyone else in knowing what is going to happen and having an answer ready.

The *reactive* Head is essentially responding to events as they occur. They determine his or her thought and actions. Work consists of dealing with manifest rather than latent problems. There never seems to be a psychological and actual time gap between what needs to be done and the need actually to do it. Over a period of time this condition creates the feeling of a treadmill existence and an inability to steer events towards the changes that are desired.

The *inactive* Head is able to let everything happen around him or her. Time is not of the essence. There is a relaxed air about him or her but this is not to be identified as casualness or indifference. He or she knows that time can be allowed to pass during which some problems can evaporate and wounds heal.

At first sight it may be tempting for every Head to consider his or her own experience and conduct in terms of one of these. It is certain that friends and colleagues would try to place the Head in one of these categories. But it is very likely that every Head demonstrates each one of these four styles in the course of a school year. The real question is which of the four tends to be dominant and whether the Head has or lacks the ability to exercise all four and to review the balance that exists between them by way of self-evaluation.

Effectiveness in headship in this regard consists of handling oneself adroitly according to need. The work of managing the school is not an undifferentiated whole. Many parts of it can look after themselves. Some parts need passing attention, others intense concentration. To be hyperactive, proactive, reactive or inactive across the whole range of work which constitutes managing the school must surely be regarded as unwise, if not slightly pathological. Rather, the Head may take careful thought about the different aspects of the work of the school and the jobs which need to be done at any particular time. From such thought it is then possible to make a sensible estimate about how to use available time. The result may be the demand for hyperactivity in one job and the application of the other time management styles variously to the other jobs. Figure 8.2 may be used for this. Items for attention as jobs to be done can be of any order. They might consist of all ten elements of the whole management task as outlined in Chapter 1. Or they might consist of a range of tasks within any one of these ten. Less likely, they might be any number of jobs which currently have to be done across a range of areas, or even within a single project or problem which engages the attention of the school.

FIGURE 8.2 Time management style analysis

Time management style needed \ Jobs to be done	1	2	3	4
Hyperactive				
Proactive				
Reactive				
Inactive				

The effective Head is one who can:
- vary the style of his or her time management
- review the balance between the different styles used
- make use of the full range of time management styles as the occasion demands

Meeting time

One of the big consumers of time is meetings. These range from the everyday casual contacts and exchanges in the corridor, hall, staffroom or wherever with colleagues, pupils and others, to the large formal gathering of staff or the parent–teacher association. Casual contacts are useful for exchanging information, finding out about development problems, becoming alert to changes in morale levels and cementing good relationships. They can all too easily lead in addition to purely socialising and therapeutic exchanges at indulgent levels. This can also apply to the use of the telephone.

If a Head is troubled about the use of time a simple remedy might be to make a conscious effort to clip 10% off the time given to everyone. This is not a damaging proportion. If a Head has been in the habit of offering an agreed amount of time to someone, it is an easy matter to offer 10% less. If time given has always been open-ended, in the mistaken belief that time is always less important than the problem, the Head should ensure the termination of the discussion as a matter of judgement as promptly as possible. Since over 54% of the primary Head's working time is said to be spent in meeting individual pupils, staff and others, a mere reduction of 10% in the allocation to each person would create a considerable amount of time for alternative use.

Formal meetings can be looked at from three points of view if the interest is in saving time. First, a particular meeting may not need to be held at all. Because it is scheduled, it does not have to be held if there is no business. In any case, there may be a cheaper and more convenient way of accomplishing what was intended by the meeting. Second, a meeting should be shown as having both a starting time and a finishing time. The latter is almost universally neglected. If an agenda is published in advance of the meeting, both times should be shown and, above all, *strictly observed*. Thirdly, within the meeting itself, proper procedures for chairing the meeting should be followed so that all the items listed on the agenda are dealt with satisfactorily. This is good for the morale of the members of the meeting as well as for the business of the school. Each item on the agenda can be marked 'for information', 'for discussion' or 'for decision' as is appropriate and the amount of time for dealing with it can also be shown on the published agenda.

Practical time savers

Good ideas can disappear from view as quickly as they come. At the time of their coming they occupy the forefront of the mind. They may become fixed there. But all too often they defy the seemingly impossible and become lost for ever. Others come and go in between pressing preoccupations. New ideas and new worries crowd out the ideas already lurking around. At a later date, time can be wasted trying to recall the idea once grasped or searching for ideas as solutions to problems. The question over saving ideas and saving time has an easy answer. Write them down as they occur. If the ideas are small ones concerning the necessary ongoing fine tuning of things already in motion, they can be put straight into the diary for systematic attention. If they are big ideas, as for a new policy or new project, they may be placed on an 'ideas list'. A queue is formed with other previous ideas awaiting consideration at the appropriate time.

Time management involves knowing oneself as well as the techniques to use. Improvement in time management can come through trial and error but it usually helps to try out time savers, perhaps one at a time, to see how they work and to become used to using them. The following are ten points to consider.

1 *Diary* — use it as an instrument of control, showing deadlines, warnings of deadlines coming up, jobs to be done and ideas which need to be thought about, carried forward day by day or week by week.
2 *Time keeping* — be punctual oneself and expect it of others in starting and ending all events in the working day.
3 *Unfinished business* — get used to living with it in the form of a whole string of jobs which are in various states of completion, each being worked on as time permits and as necessity demands.
4 *Regular habits of work* — do a little to one or more jobs in the pipeline every day; it amounts to a lot of work over a few weeks. Bear in mind that the favourable block of time for doing something is the ideal which never really materialises and can be the excuse for procrastination.
5 *Small targets* — select a modest amount to do in a particular period of limited time. Actually doing it is good for morale, whereas setting the sights on doing too much at once is likely to be unfulfilling and counterproductive.
6 *Concentration on the job in hand* — it is not always necessary to down tools every time something comes up. Doing this can be a cloak for relief from the task in hand. Perhaps what has come up can wait or can be given attention by someone else. Everyone else can soon become habituated to interrupting the Head at any time over any issue if the Head lets it be known that he or she is — and is seen to be — infinitely accessible.

7   *Written brevity* — confining as many items of school business as possible in all fields, when in written form, to one side of A4 and getting others to do the same. People are more likely to read short papers properly.

8   *Best hours for working* — using them regularly for doing the most important or difficult jobs, even if it is before breakfast. Jobs which seem mountainous at the time of the Head's worst hours for working seem to be quite modest at the time of the best hours. On tackling the job, especially if it is written work, go straight to it, avoiding pencil sharpening or cups of coffee.

9   *Despatch* — if in doubt, do it now. Many tasks involve far too much time through being picked up and put down again with nothing added. Multiple handling of jobs needs to be avoided. If a paper comes to hand or a job comes up, it should be despatched instantly wherever possible.

10 *Keeping fit* — overtiredness or rash indulgences do not aid the good management of time.

Postscript on time management

There can be a penalty in being expert in making the most of time. Anyone who is reliable, prompt and on top of the job becomes an automatic target for others who want something done. The upshot of good time management is to make more and more room to meet increasing requests for favours, help, consultancy and advice. This becomes a particular danger in the case of those who are reluctant or unable to say 'no' to others.

But the far greater danger comes from within oneself. As the efficiency levels of time management improve, room is created to take on more commitments of one's own seeking. The ultimate effect is that everything becomes too finely poised and too sensitive to the unexpected. The odd mishap, holdup or bout of ill-health can throw personal work into chaos.There is a limit to what anyone can sustain. To push beyond those limits, lured there by successively successful adaptations made in the management of time, is the ultimate folly.

9

Working with the deputy head

Most Heads of primary schools have been deputy heads of primary schools. It is the customary post to hold previous to becoming Head. Holders of deputy headship posts are normally expected to consider becoming Heads. The majority do try to obtain headship posts at one time or another, though in recent years fewer have succeeded as the total number of primary schools in the country has declined. If a school is too small to warrant a deputy head's post as such, an experienced teacher usually acts as the Head's deputy and such a teacher is entitled to apply direct for the headship of a small school.

The practice of presuming that deputy heads form the pool from which to appoint new Heads of school is justified for two reasons. In the first place, a teacher promoted to deputy headship usually achieves it on the basis of exceptional performance as a teacher. But, secondly, a deputy head is supposed to have more insight into what is involved in being head of school than other staff. If the Head is so minded, his or her deputy can have a rich and varied set of opportunities to learn the job of being Head. It is not uncommon, however, for Heads to exercise a restrictive attitude towards their deputies. They have little or no access to school business other than what is available to the staff in general. They are not made party to information which is available and problems which are appearing in advance of the time when everybody on the staff is invited to know about them.

In extreme cases there may be nothing special about being deputy head beyond being nominally in charge during the Head's absence from the school premises. Otherwise, the deputy head is virtually a full-time class teacher with an implied, if not explicit, demand to be the best teacher in the school and an example to other staff. In this task he or she can fall victim to misunderstanding over the nature and status of deputy headship. On being rebuked by her deputy head for inadequate discipline, the teacher concerned replied in a fit of pique: 'It's all right for you — the children do what you tell them to because you're the deputy head'. But this only drew out the following rejoinder from the deputy: 'No, you're wrong. I am deputy head because the children do what I tell them'.

In contrast, the deputy head can be enabled to take a very full part in the school beyond the classroom to the point of genuinely sharing in its overall management. Such enabling is almost entirely at the discretion of the Head. The school's governors may or may not have a view about it. But clearly, much depends on the attitude, competence and willingness of the particular deputy head.

The deputy head as an asset

From the Head's point of view a good deputy can be an inestimable asset. Being a 'good deputy' in this context means two things — that the Head and deputy get along well together at the personal level and that the deputy turns out to be effective at any job he or she undertakes. Being head of school can be a lonely experience. The nature of the job itself is to some extent isolating. But for some Heads it is self-imposed. The top job, however, need not lie that heavily on anybody.

Some Heads thoroughly enjoy being boss and seem to flourish without needing to cultivate and rely on others for support and sustenance. The danger is that if they exhibit a style which is too autocratic, others will feel left out and the chief casualty could be the deputy head. In contrast, some Heads find it hard to exercise the executive task and feel a strong need to develop a substantial network of supporting associates among the staff and elsewhere. In any case, some people are more naturally friendly than others. But the danger here is that extensive deference to others may be felt to be necessary. The Head's position may become compromised, leading to an inability to make critical decisions and to take decisive action.

For staff up to the level of deputy head there is always the hope that the head of school is an understanding, sympathetic and supportive colleague. But who sustains the Head? There is an expectation perhaps that those who become Heads are somehow able to sustain themselves — to bear their responsibilities with fortitude and equanimity and still to have enough emotional and spiritual strength left over to help and sustain others. In practice this can be far from the case. A high degree of self-reliance and self-assurance does exist among Heads but this is increasingly found to be inadequate without some kind of resource beyond the personal ones. It is true that Heads have access to members of the local education authority's advisory or inspectorial staff. But the appearance of so many spontaneously formed mutual support groups by Heads themselves in a locality underlines their feeling of vulnerability. Many have the feeling that in contemporary society they are expected to be above reproach and that they cannot admit to failure or having any shortcomings.

If such negative feelings govern the relationship between the Head and his or her deputy in school, a relaxed and productive working relationship between the two will surely be prevented. It is fortunate if the Head and deputy get along well together — such a relationship may obviate the need to search for relief and support elsewhere. But too frequently such a relationship does not exist. One chief adviser is on record as saying, that when the local education authority concerned ran separate courses for Heads and deputy heads on a problem solving basis, it was frequently found that the prevalent problem was that the Head could not get along with his or her deputy or vice versa.

The degree of liking or disliking a close colleague may vary, but normally falls within a range which does not affect being able to work together on the basis of a cordial and responsible professional relationship. If a colleague is liked — particularly the Head — the chances of that person proving to be effective are potentially increased. If disliked, the potential for ineffectiveness is increased. Strictly speaking, professional life ought to be above personal liking and disliking: an objective reality ought to prevail. But in the close society of a primary school this is not easy to accomplish. Personal regard and disregard may obtrude to become a contaminating influence.

The deputy head, like the Head and other members of staff, is paid as an employee to carry out certain work and to do so in co-operation with others for whom, sometimes, there may be little or no regard. Junior staff, for their part, need to understand that the work of the Head is sooner or later bound to involve a measure of unpopularity. He or she will seek to be effective by managing the school objectively: this should guarantee the respect of staff, if not increase their personal liking for the Head.

Staff can like a Head as a person but deplore his or her managerial ability. Alternatively, they can recognise the managerial competence of the Head in terms of the welfare and prosperity of the school without much personal liking. Staff can forgive a Head for not being a particularly winsome and likeable personality but not for failing to manage the school effectively.

This is the context within which the relationships between the Head and the deputy head must be forged. It is delicate territory. If good relationships can be established, a deputy head with high motivation and job satisfaction can be an enormous asset to the Head and to the whole school. If these are not achieved, numerous difficulties may be added to the array of tasks which make up the management of the school. The effective Head is one who has worked out a relationship and way of working with the deputy which is acceptable to both.

Basis for the Head/deputy relationship

The leadership of the Head, as discussed in Chapter 3, can be demonstrated at its best in the case of relating to the deputy head. Many Heads, however, do not approach their relationship with their deputy heads on a constructive basis. The assumption is that the deputy is justifying his or her job by being the 'errand boy', the 'intermediary' or the 'eyes and ears' of the Head.

It is possible to classify the many different relationships found in practice. The 'frustration relationship' is where the deputy is keen to engage in wider responsibilities than his or her own immediate teaching duties but finds that the Head continually reserves all the business of managing the school for himself or herself. The result of this may be to throw the deputy irrecoverably into a state of apathy. If there is at the same time any alienation among the staff, it may exacerbate a staff-versus-the-Head situation. The deputy's frustration is increased if the Head is not only possessive about school business but is less than competent in discharging it, especially if the deputy's views are either not sought, or, if sought, then ignored.

The 'authority relationship' can spring from the Head's secret fear of losing personal control of the school and being compared unfavourably with the deputy head. Or it can arise when the deputy is perceived to be incompetent and undeserving of special consideration and only warranting minimal recognition. The relationship is dominated by the directiveness of the Head. Any tasks undertaken by the deputy are one-off; they are without delegated authority and responsibility over a period of time.

The 'change relationship' is where the Head expects the deputy to act as executive, carrying into practical effect the changes he or she as Head wants to see in the school. In other words, the Head, having decided the policy, makes the deputy head responsible for implementing it. The changes may be trivial or substantial. They may in fact be difficult to achieve, calling for great powers of persuasion and constant hard work on the part of the deputy, who may have had little or no say in what the changes were to be. He or she is essentially the executive.

The 'collegial relationship' fully involves the deputy head in the business of the school. He or she is made party to information as it is received and to problems as they arise. There is continual discussion between Head and deputy over what steps might be taken. A good deal of trust and interpersonal rapport is developed through working together and making an effort.

Certain stereotypes can be used to capture the flavour of these four models, as follows:[16]

1 The frustration relationship
   sergeant major   top of the 'other ranks' but never the officer though probably able to do the job equally well
2 The authority relationship
   aide-de-camp   one who carries the orders to others and sees they are carried out but never originates them
3 The change relationship
   managing director conforms to the policy of the chairman of the board of directors, carrying out changes required with the exercise of wide powers and skills

4   The collegial relationship
partner   partner of the collaborative — not legal — kind,
                                working together on all aspects of the school's bus-
                                iness

An important factor governing the relationship between Head and
deputy head in the primary school is the former's assumptions about the
strategic and tactical aspects of management. Strategy is about broader
goals and the different kinds of action needed. This can be approached
by the synoptic route — extensive and overall planning — or by the
incremental route — piecemeal and pragmatic development. Every Head
will wish to specify his or her own responsibilities accordingly, and derive
what the deputy head should do from them. But clearly, if the synoptic
route is chosen, there would seem to be more scope for the deputy to
take part in higher level work than if the Head chooses the incremental
route.

Tactics is about reaching short term objectives within a more general
set of goals or strategy. The higher the office the more necessary it is to
become involved in strategic thinking and action as opposed to tactical
thinking and action. On the face of it, therefore, there are reasonable
grounds for a division of labour between the Head and deputy. In this
connection, it is often said of a school that if the deputy head left the
school would collapse overnight but if the Head left no-one would notice.
Conversely, where it is said that, if the Head left, the school would
collapse overnight but if the deputy-head left no-one would notice, the
same kind of honourable conclusion may be drawn. In each case, one is
good with the strategic thinking and action, the other is good with the
tactical thinking and action. Of course, in each case the dishonourable
conclusion may also be drawn that one of the two is very ineffective,
with the result that the other shoulders both kinds of work for the school.
It may be added that though the school notices the absence of the tactical
manager very soon, the absence of the strategic manager, though less
dramatically felt, would be noticed just as surely and more profoundly
over time.

Division of work

There are two ways of looking at the division of work between the Head
and the deputy head in a primary school. One is by making a catalogue
of jobs each can do. Another is by ensuring complementary strengths in
the way of working so that management is effective as a result of team
effort. The actual work carried out by the deputy head might be viewed
as one side of a division of work with the Head. This can be arrived at
by agreement between the two or as a fiat from the Head. The jobs then
undertaken by the deputy might be fully delegated — that is, he or she

may carry them out in the way thought best, with the freedom to make mistakes. Or, the same jobs might be carried out under variable degrees of direction from the Head.

In addition, they might all or in part be subject to job rotation. In other words, the Head and deputy might agree a division of jobs between them for one year or some other suitable period of time and exchange them the following year. One reason for doing this could be relief from tedious jobs and the need for fresh motivation. It provides opportunity for jobs to be understood in more depth and extends the managerial competence in the school. It incidentally gives the deputy an invaluable range of experience antecedent to his or her own headship. Such a rotation needs to take into account the deputy's ability and seniority but responsibilities can be increased as the Head thinks fit every time the job rotation comes up for renewal. At these points there are rich grounds for offering the deputy an appraisal.

In theory, as in the following example, nothing need be precluded from such a job rotation arrangement. In practice, however, there may be good reasons for limiting the range of jobs which are included in it, notably if the deputy has a full-time teaching load.

One Head's list of tasks in a division of work with the deputy head in a primary school was as follows:[17]

Head	*Deputy head*
Curriculum	Budget
Ethos	Day-to-day
Evaluation	Discipline of pupils
External	Extramural activities
Long term planning	Internal
Management of pupils	Junior staff
Policy	Lower school
Senior staff	Non-teaching staff
Teaching staff	Pastoral
Timetabling	Resources
Upper school	Routines
Whole community	School community

The second way of looking at the division of work between the Head and deputy is focused elsewhere than on discrete jobs which each can do. In the management of the primary school it is most helpful to have available certain types of skill which can be applied to any particular job if a strong team effort is needed. These skills mark out the contribution that each person can bring to bear on the management activity of the school at large. They are a reflection of temperament and propensities and are concerned more with how a person tends to go about his or her work than with the identity of the work itself.

The argument runs along these lines. Management makes many-sided demands. Effective management requires the exercise of a certain number of skills. It is unlikely that all of them can be found in sufficient measure in one person who, in any case, would not have the time to use them all properly if he or she did possess them all in sufficient measure. The case exists, therefore, for unifying the skills found among two or more people. This is the process of creating and building team management.

Eight such skills have been found to exist and to be necessary in practice.[18]

1 The 'organising skill': being able to get things going so that the desired effect or change is actually understood and striven for. It involves having a capacity for enlisting help, creating co-operation, and knowing what is possible. This implies being able to generate interest and effort.

2 The 'chairing skill': being able to apply the technical rules and procedures in a dispassionate manner, so that any meeting is orderly and productive in terms of its intended purpose. It involves being able to bring out the best contributions of every member of the meeting.

3 The 'shaping skill': being able to drive for the completion of tasks. This involves drawing attention to what is to be done, the objectives that are needed and suggestions for speeding up the work.

4 The 'provoking skill': being able to advance new ideas, unorthodox solutions to problems or ways of doing things. It is being peculiarly able to suggest ways out of an impasse, challenging traditional thinking and pointing out snags and obstacles not being taken into account.

5 The 'investigating skill': being able to find out the location and nature of resources which are actually or potentially useful, including information, materials and contacts. This is a preoccupation which is coupled with a classifying kind of mind and perhaps a good filing system.

6 The 'evaluating skill': being able to weigh up problems and proposed solutions, analysing ideas and suggestions. It is able to indicate and clarify their meaning for the school so that better decisions can be made.

7 The 'finishing skill': being able to give attention to detail both in advance of implementation and more particularly during the implementation of an idea or scheme. It involves maintaining the urgency of the team's work and stressing the demand for precision and accuracy.

8 The 'leading skill': being able to get a team to cohere. It brings out the strengths of members and supports their weaknesses, building communications between the members, fostering team spirit and neutralising differences which may crop up between them.

These skills could be taken into account by the Head in thinking about his or her relationships with the deputy head. They offer a different basis for instituting a division of work from that of actual jobs undertaken. If the abilities and respective strengths of the Head and deputy are fully and mutually recognised, there can be a sound foundation for building a team. Such a division would need to be among more than two if the team is to be larger. These abilities also provide a framework for assessing the deputy's professional progress and development.

Postscript on working with the deputy head

It is of vital interest to the school to have a good deputy head. Nothing can spoil the Head's ambitions for the school and sour relationships among the staff more, than a deputy who is disappointing at his or her job, or who is at loggerheads with the staff or alienated from the Head. In contrast, if the deputy's contribution to the school is cultivated carefully, his or her drive, good relationships, enthusiasm, hard work and loyalty can enhance the school's prosperity.

From the deputy head's own standpoint, to do an effective job, and to be enabled to have as much experience of management as possible, are usually sources of job satisfaction. For those who are seeking headship, there is extra motivation for doing a good job but normally, whatever the situation, a deputy head ought to give the Head as much consideration and support as possible. The Head reciprocally needs to express to the deputy head his or her appreciation, to offer encouragement and support and to show tolerance. Regularly, the two of them should undertake constructive and critical reviews of their professional relationship and their joint work on behalf of the school.

10

Taking professional stock

It is easy in teaching to be so busy with the job that there is little inclination and no priority to take stock. Every Head needs to take stock from time to time. Part of being effective is the habit of taking stock — of plans in progress and developments being implemented, but above all of one's own professional achievements and interests.

Perspectives for taking professional stock may be limited to examining one's own managerial performance. The task is then a matter of deciding on the performance indicators to be used and what measure on each is acceptable. This is never easy to do since individual Heads vary so much in their ambitions and satisfaction levels. For example, if 'new project starts' is adopted as one performance indicator for effective headship, some Heads may consider that two in a year are highly satisfactory, while others may consider five in a year to be highly satisfactory. Much depends, in any case, on the nature of the particular school concerned and its circumstances.

There are other perspectives, however, for the Head to use in taking stock. Although managerial performance remains inevitably the main focus, other perspectives need to be given some attention in relation to it. In this chapter a method for rating overall managerial performance is introduced; it will be followed by a consideration of these other perspectives.

Personal management performance review

It is to be hoped that every Head of a primary school retains an outstanding capacity for classroom teaching. In the case of teaching Heads this is demonstrated on a daily basis. In the case of non-teaching Heads their capacity can be regularly demonstrated when they cover for other staff or seek to retain a teaching slot in the programme. Staff are thus able to witness and appreciate the Head's own subject knowledge and mastery of method. They may readily seek or accept the Head's advice and comments on their own teaching. If the Head seldom teaches, his or her capacity to do so may materially decline.

It is, however, to the effective management of the school that staff sooner or later look when they contemplate the professional performance of their Head. To some extent deficiencies in executive capacity may receive some compensation in the minds of staff if the Head is outstanding and energetic in the teaching sphere. But such a deficiency must surely register as an absolute shortcoming in the minds of those outside the school.

As with teaching in the classroom itself, the Head is able to have direct and indirect feedback about his or her managerial work. Children may express their pleasure about particular events or activities. Staff may show their appreciation of arrangements made for them individually or collectively. Parents, governors and the wider public may make favourable comments about the school in general or a particular event or a feature of it. Advisory or inspectorial staff from the local education authority may pass complimentary remarks about initiatives taken. Other Heads may begin to regard the school highly and say so. Of course, criticisms as well as compliments may come from many of these people.

In such a build-up of indicators, the Head needs to take notice of negative signs — what is *not said* — as well as positive information — *what is actually said*. The effective Head is one who is mindful that flattery and the transmission of selective information are commonplace and should be separated from the sober, objective views and reviews that are required to manage a school. All sorts of people may want to please the Head, to offer praise on one issue in order to draw attention away from another issue and to store up a measure of goodwill with the Head for future reference. Sincere praise is welcome, but a touch of scepticism about one's own performance is more valuable.

The test is always whether or not the school is moving to the fulfilment of its own objectives. If this is happening and others are saying so, so much the better. The supremacy of objectives for the school and the need not to be deflected from them are illustrated in the following contrasting cases, concerning two adjacent primary schools in the same metropolitan district authority.

In one school, strict discipline, formal teaching, quiet and orderly conduct, obedience and regimentation reigned. Many people both inside and outside the teaching profession openly or secretly deplored many of its features. Visitors to the authority to see its schools were never taken to see this particular school. It was not considered to be quite in vogue.

The second school was all that the first was not. It was full of working noise, very informal in operation, and organised in open plan areas with individualised and group work. The visual work of the children was vast in quantity and of a high standard, lavishly displayed around the school. 'Progressive' teachers and others were fond of visiting this school and the authority was always pleased to encourage such visitors and to draw attention to it as its showpiece or shopwindow school.

The first school, however, had a firm place as the authority's backroom school. When the time came for interschool or national competitions and the exhibition of achievements in knowledge or skill, such as music, it was to this school that the authority turned.

Insofar as each school was reaching its own objectives, they were equally meritorious.

Management performance profile

Workaday feedback may be sufficient for the Head to use in reviewing his or her own managerial performance. But it can be too intermittent, too patchy and too unreliable to provide a consistent picture of the entire range of work performance. Where this is so a more systematic, inclusive and deliberate approach can be made at the Head's own initiative.

Presented below is one possible way of doing this. It is based on the model of management for the primary school, seen as a composite task, presented in Chapter 1. The Head completes the process for himself or herself. This is the basic exercise of taking stock. But it may also be helpful if the Head asks others to complete it on him or her. In this way, self-perceptions can be compared with those of working colleagues who are on the receiving end of the Head's managerial conduct and actions. It cannot be expected that the Head should be outstanding at everything. The end product of the process therefore is a management performance profile. This shows a range of results in which the Head can see what his or her overall performance is in a particular school at a particular time. The profile may then be used as a reference for an action programme to improve performance in selected areas as needed.

MANAGEMENT PERFORMANCE PROFILE:
HEAD OF PRIMARY SCHOOL

The material used has been developed with the help of a substantial number of senior staff in primary schools. It has been tested for acceptability and applicability with primary school Heads.

Purpose and features

The purpose of this material is to provide a basis for you to assess the scope and level of your own managerial performance as Head of a primary school. In addition, you may complement your own perceptions of your work by asking any number of other Heads, or members of the teaching or non-teaching staff of your school, to assess *your work* as Head of your school, by completing this material about you.

Terms used

The following special terms are used:

Managerial performance categories	These are ten major areas for assessing performance, taken from Figure 1.2 in Chapter 1.
Managerial performance items	These are 100 specific examples for assessing performance within these categories; there are ten for each category.
Managerial performance zones	These are the main orientations which performance may have in practice. There are two zones, each subsuming five managerial performance categories.

Steps

There are *four* steps for dealing with this material. Each should be completed in the order given.

Step 1

To make the interpretation of the results as meaningful as possible, you should first assign a weighting or order of priority to the ten managerial performance categories listed below. The idea is that you should indicate the importance you attach to each in the school where you are currently working as Head.

Rank order these ten managerial performance categories
Use as your criterion: How critical is each category for establishing and maintaining my effectiveness?
Put 1 for the *most* critical, 2 for the next most critical, and so on, putting 10 for the least critical of them all.

Managerial performance categories	*Rank order numbers*
Physical assets	––––––––––––––
School climate	––––––––––––––
Values and objectives	––––––––––––––
Curriculum content and development	––––––––––––––
Organisation, care and development of children	––––––––––––––
Staff structure and deployment	––––––––––––––
Financial and systems management	––––––––––––––
Standards of performance	––––––––––––––
External relations	––––––––––––––
Managerial skills	––––––––––––––

Step 2

The main part of the process is to estimate your own performance level for each and every one of 100 selected specific items. These are representative of all the areas in the range of management conduct and activities. The ratings you give are relative to one another. They are also relative to the standard of performance you may wish to set yourself. A five-point rating scale is suggested. This should be *fully* used to indicate differences between the items.

Rate the following 100 personal managerial performance items on a 1–5 scale.
1 is least effective
5 most effective
2,3 and 4 are intermediate ratings.
Enter the rating number which best represents your performance on the right. *Every item should be rated.*

1	Reading professional literature	....
2	Establishing clear objectives for all areas of the curriculum	....
3	Creating and maintaining efficient pupil records	....
4	Visiting classroom/teaching areas during teaching time	....
5	Looking and thinking ahead	....
6	Enabling children to be happy at school	....
7	Encouraging the versatility of staff through job rotation	....
8	Having up-to-date knowledge of the staff's work in progress	....
9	Promoting my own innovations	....
10	Identifying the needs of individual children	....
11	Listening to new suggestions and discussing them	....
12	Having knowledge of the school's curriculum	....
13	Reporting back to staff from external meetings, conferences and courses	....
14	Providing an extra-curricular programme	....
15	Taking corrective steps when performance levels fall	....
16	Planning the curriculum as a progression throughout the school	....
17	Providing for children with special needs	....
18	Reviewing staff members' work performance with them	....
19	Allocating space and facilities fairly and avoiding accommodation clashes and confusion	....
20	Making calm and considered decisions	....
21	Having a sense of humour	....
22	Being persuasive	....
23	Establishing informal working relationships with staff	....
24	Having knowledge of the location of materials and equipment	....
25	Making the school a comfortable and attractive place of work	....
26	Being approachable and trustworthy	....
27	Holding workshops and other events to promote school–home links	....
28	Providing a secure and calm environment for children	....
29	Securing the good decorative state of the school	....
30	Making known to all staff the administrative procedures required by the local education authority	....
31	Suggesting new ways of teaching to staff	....
32	Raising additional resources for the school	....
33	Ensuring that agreed initiatives are properly resourced	....
34	Making appointments with parents and keeping them	....

35 Having clarity, brevity and accuracy in written documents ....

36 Ensuring everything is in safe condition and good repair ....

37 Drawing attention to educational theory and practice elsewhere ....

38 Anticipating problems staff may have ....

39 Carrying responsibility without stress ....

40 Involving the governors in school developments ....

41 Encouraging teachers with unusual knowledge and skills to use them in the curriculum ....

42 Making the best use of time ....

43 Engaging the staff in INSET outside and inside the school ....

44 Welcoming new families to the school ....

45 Using teaching accommodation fully and appropriately ....

46 Organising paperwork systems in the school ....

47 Regulating the access and movement of children into, within and around the school ....

48 Encouraging courteous and open dealings between staff and children ....

49 Drawing the attention of staff to the need for career development ....

50 Encouraging staff to vary their teaching methods ....

51 Making firm decisions on the distribution of resources ....

52 Knowing each child by name ....

53 Facing a difficulty or crisis ....

54 Maintaining discipline ....

55 Relating to children in a positive way ....

56 Involving staff in the wider problems and events of school life ....

57 Adapting the structure of the school organisation ....

58 Seeing that the school office is well organised ....

59 Encouraging happy, effective and critical co-operation ....

60 Persuading the local community to help the school ....

61 Using school assemblies to set the tone of the school ....

62 Making full use of facilities and equipment ....

63 Emphasising the importance of setting and reaching objectives ....

64 Being prompt and accurate in business matters ....

65 Making firm decisions on disciplinary matters concerning staff and children ....

66 Suggesting themes or topics to teaching staff ....

67 Conducting regular sessions to review the curriculum ....

68 Withholding promotion from incompetent staff ....

69 Discussing policy and working well with the deputy head ....

70 Making the school available for community use ....

71 Gauging staff abilities and potential ....

72 Publishing and enforcing school rules ....

73 Cultivating responsibility, creativity and initiative in children ....

74 Keeping the caretaker and secretary informed of scheduled events ....

75 Knowing where to get extra resources outside the school ....

76 Providing opportunities for the development of social awareness in children ....

77 Making all needed apparatus, materials and equipment for teaching purposes available ....

78 Delegating responsibilities ....

79 Reviewing the standard of children's work regularly with staff ....

80 Developing a school association for parents, friends and teachers ....

81 Praising good work in staff and children ....

82 Working for the reputation of the school through activities with other Heads, other professional and local bodies and the local education authority ....

83 Eliciting staff participation in setting objectives and planning ....

84 Encouraging new ideas and experimentation ....

85 Having a working staff development policy ....

86 Achieving clean and tidy conditions in all parts of the school ....

87 Signposting the school inside and out ....

88 Making the most of limited finances ....

89 Dealing with advisers, inspectors and governors ....

90 Displaying children's work ....

91 Reiterating the school's organisational mission objectives often ....

92 Conducting regular overall school reviews ....

93 Agreeing precise job descriptions ....

94 Inviting and integrating parental help in the school ....

95 Encouraging children to work hard ....

96 Making a regular teaching contribution ....

97 Producing and circulating agreed outline curricula ....

98 Devoting staff meeting time to curricular matters ....

99 Keeping a regular check on children's work ....

100 Having a sound grasp of the school's finances ....

Step 3

Transfer the ratings you have given for the 100 personal managerial performance items to the appropriate places below and total up the ten managerial performance categories ready for step 4. Each total will be not less than 10 and not more than 50 (reference the rating scale of 1–5 on each item).

It will be seen in Step 3 that the 100 items between them represent the ten managerial performance categories in step 1.

Physical assets

Item No	Rating
24	
25	
29	
36	
45	
62	
77	
86	
87	
90	
Total	

School climate

Item No	Rating
19	
21	
23	
26	
39	
48	
56	
59	
61	
65	
Total	

Values and objectives

Item No	Rating
2	
4	
9	
13	
18	
63	
72	
83	
91	
92	
Total	

Curriculum content and development

Item No	Rating
1	
12	
14	
16	
31	
66	
67	
84	
97	
98	
Total	

Organisation, care and development of children

Item No	Rating
6	
10	
17	
28	
47	
52	
54	
55	
73	
76	
Total	

Staff structure and deployment

Item No	Rating
7	
38	
41	
43	
49	
50	
57	
68	
71	
93	
Total	

Financial and systems management

Item No	Rating
30	
32	
33	
46	
51	
58	
64	
74	
88	
100	
Total	

Standards of performance

Item No	Rating
3	
8	
15	
37	
79	
81	
85	
95	
96	
99	
Total	

External relations

Item No	Rating
27	
34	
40	
44	
60	
70	
75	
80	
82	
94	
Total	

Managerial skills

Item No	Rating
5	
11	
20	
22	
35	
42	
53	
69	
78	
89	
Total	

Step 4

The final step consists of making use of the results. This may be done with the help of Figure 10.1.

FIGURE 10.1   A primary Head's management performance profile

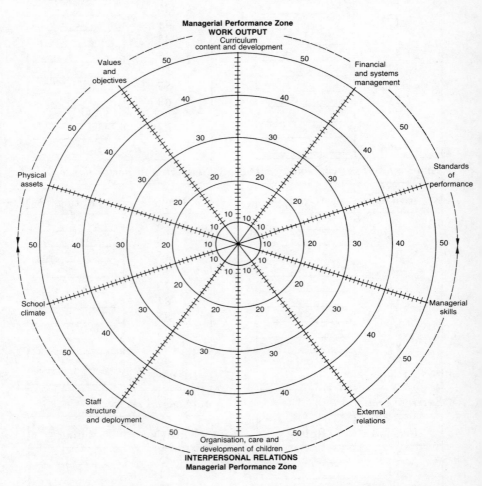

1   Take your ten totals and mark each in turn onto its own radius of the circle.
2   Join up all ten points that you have marked. The resulting shape gives you your management performance profile at a glance.

Managerial performance zones

The five managerial performance categories located in the upper half of the circle may be viewed as being primarily oriented towards

work output

The five managerial performance categories located in the lower half of the circle may be viewed as being primarily oriented towards

interpersonal relations

Final points to note
Your personal management performance profile may be considered from four points of view:

1   In which managerial performance categories could I do *better*?
2   What is the *strength* of my performance in each of the two managerial performance zones?
3   Is there a *balance* between the two managerial performance zones?
4   Consider the results in the light of the *relative importance* you attached to each category in step 1.

Note
If you have also asked others to rate your performance, process their ratings in the same way. A comparison of the Management Performance Profiles produced by their ratings may be made with yours. This will show the extent of agreement between your own perceptions and those who are subject to your management or who can observe it in action.

In interpreting the results it is necessary to bear in mind that each of the ten scores needs to be seen in relation to the others. There may be one or two disappointing results out of the ten. The areas they represent clearly might be given remedial attention. However, all ten results — whether strong or weak in relation to the others — when taken together may represent *either* a good *or* a poor managerial performance *in relation to the school's needs*. Hopefully, a Head can be objective enough to make his or her ratings honestly and thoughtfully. If others have been asked to assess the Head, their results should throw light upon the Head's managerial performance in terms of the school's needs as perceived by them. A Head may rate himself or herself more highly than is warranted or lower than is warranted; obtaining assessments from others offers a corrective or a corroboration.

Professional review

The first of the other perspectives for taking stock is closely related to managerial performance. This is professional review. It consists of two elements — teaching expertise and managing expertise. It is a matter of debate as to which of the two is the more important. It is a matter of balance, with the balance tilting in favour of the latter — at least in all but the smallest schools.

As far as the teaching element is concerned, the Head, like any other teacher, needs to keep abreast of developments in his or her subject fields — in regard to both content and methods of teaching. To do this will probably include the need to read books and journals, to attend courses and to belong to specialist associations. The smaller the school and the greater the Head's own teaching commitments in it, the more he or she may feel the need to keep regularly in touch with developments elsewhere. The larger the school and the smaller the Head's commitment to regular and substantial teaching duties, the greater the temptation to make do with existing expertise. This may seem a necessary sacrifice in order to give full attention to the second element — the managerial or executive task.

The Head's managerial expertise needs the same high standard of attention and consideration that can be given to teaching expertise. It has to be maintained and nurtured in the same way. This too can be accomplished by reading books and specialist journals, belonging to appropriate professional associations, talking with other Heads, attending conferences, and enlisting on short specialist courses or master's degree courses (MEd and MSc) which are on offer in various parts of the country. Attention is drawn to the model short course outline provided as an Appendix.

Just as teaching improvement is reflected in the use of updated material and methods, so on the managing side the endeavour to improve one's expertise should be reflected in practice or performance. Here are some of the more important items in which, after taking stock, improved expertise might be needed.

1   addressing various groups and large audiences
2   being an efficient administrator — using time well
3   appraisal interviewing
4   chairing meetings
5   counselling
6   communicating — accuracy, precision, promptness
7   decision making — decision building techniques and decisiveness
8   encouraging effort and enterprise in others
9   evaluating — as a systematic process
10   giving praise and constructive criticism
11   handling irate people
12   interviewing — parents, staff for appointments
13   improving knowledge — up-to-dateness, relevance, remembering, retrieval
14   using flexible leadership style
15   organising — clarity, simplicity
16   reviewing staff participation — adjusting levels sensitively

17   planning — thinking things through in advance
18   preparing — being ahead of deadlines
19   reporting — verbal or written: accuracy, conciseness
20   training — staff in general, deputy head in particular

A number of these managerial skills apply to teaching in the classroom but they are also exercised by the Head in a different dimension and at a different level. Taken together, these 20 items make up a powerful range of skills needed for the effective management of the school. It is unlikely that any Head — even the most effective — can be outstanding in performance in every one of these. But there is sufficiently varied expertise required — challenging every Head who wants to take stock — to map out a continuous programme of self-development.

Anticipation is a key factor. Waiting until one finds out that there is a serious deficiency in one's range of skills is an ineffective strategy. Being alert to the demands of the job and one's own strengths, when combined with serious attempts to correct deficiencies is, in contrast, an effective strategy. By it, much stress and many mistakes can be avoided. Learning on the job and through the job is probably the best method for learning about many jobs. But as far as headship is concerned, this must imply taking active steps to raise performance levels above those which currently exist. Otherwise, experience will turn out to be simply a demonstration and repetition of skill at a static level of competence.

A particular skill may be picked out each year for special development. This might include some practice of it in private — observing oneself in the mirror or listening to oneself on tape — and reading about it, attending a short course on it, observing others in action and discussing it with a professional friend.

Project management review

Project management review consists of looking at the number and kind of projects which the Head is managing directly or indirectly. This may be accomplished by classifying them into the following categories:
- projects completed
- projects started but not completed
- projects waiting to be started

A project in this context means any managerial initiative by the Head. It is not to be confused with curriculum topics/projects which teaching staff engage in with children. Management projects may be large or small and of any kind whatsoever. The criterion is that a project is something going on over a period of time and occupying the thought, attention and action of either a few or many persons. All such projects certainly fall into the ten categories described in Chapter 1, which between them make up the range of management work for the Head of the primary school. They can vary much in scope and scale from clearing out and cleaning up cupboards, corridors, corners and rooms of the school to a major curriculum reform or a programme involving the local community.

In taking stock through a management project review, it may be judged that the school has absorbed enough initiatives for the time being, or, perhaps, has not been able to absorb them sufficiently to warrant a period of rest and consolidation (with reference to the 'supporting' and 'stabilising' leadership styles described in Chapter 3). Or it may be the case that enough projects are currently in motion to occupy the attention and energies of the school fully for the time being so that any further projects must await a more suitable time.

It is to be noted that for the purpose of taking stock, the Head needs to take account not only of those projects for which he or she is personally responsible but also all the other projects which he or she has authorised. Together, they represent to the staff, children and the wider community the school's total work load, much or all of which may be in addition to the regular teaching.

This perspective on taking stock is importantly connected with the Head's chances of being effective and being seen to be effective. Most of a Head's working day is spent in unseen, unsung and unexceptional activity. This is doubtless the basis for effective headship, when the work is thoroughly and consistently carried out; it is the unrelieved toil necessary to keep things going. It is difficult for others to comprehend all that is entailed and it is certainly difficult to dramatise it. It probably amounts to 80% of of the Head's job content/work output *in terms of time spent*. But it is the other 20% that is most likely to make an impact on others, particularly those outside the school, who are going to make judgements about the Head's quality of leadership. So it is necessary to make the most of the 20% by seizing opportunities or manufacturing them in order to create an impact on others. Since effectiveness is by its very nature so much the gift of others, this minority time, if adroitly used, can well repay the attention and energy given. This implies being alert to chance happenings with individuals or groups as well as instigating deliberate events inside and outside the school.

Career development

A further perspective for taking stock is overall career development. Some Heads of primary schools arrive in their posts late in their teaching careers and are happy to see the remaining years until retirement taken up with discharging the headship task. Others assume headship at an earlier age and may not regard remaining in the headship of the same school until retirement as the final fulfilment of their teaching careers. They may in fact not regard headship itself as the final kind of work they want to do. Many Heads seek promotion to the headship of larger schools or different work in the education system — mainly in the advisory and inspectorial service of local education authorities, or in Her Majesty's Inspectorate, or in higher education — working in teacher education and training.

Taking stock, if thoroughly done, can include a consideration of long term career directions and objectives. This is something which many teachers neglect, being preoccupied with immediate concerns — the content and method of their class teaching and their pastoral responsibility for children. The years quickly pass while they strive to increase and maintain their competence and adequacy in the job. Little thought may be given as to how they see themselves in future years. Those who, in complete contrast, seem to be endlessly absorbed in such thoughts are often regarded as overly ambitious to the point of distraction.

It is, however, neither unnatural nor yet unseemly to give some thought to career development on a rational basis. Such a consideration of future positions, jobs and authority can serve as a healthy stimulus. Some teachers become Heads as it were by default, but most do so as a result of sustained effort.

At the outset of a career in teaching and at periodic intervals, taking stock from the point of view of career development needs to be undertaken. This applies to Heads of primary schools, large numbers of whom fall into the 35–45 age bracket. Taking stock for this group in particular may be undertaken by considering the following questions with a view to obtaining some honest answers.

1   Do I wish to continue as Head of this school?
2   If so, what ought I to do to guarantee
    a   becoming effective?
    or
    b   continuing to be effective?
3   Am I prepared to make any changes in my private life which may be necessary to make this possible?
4   Do I wish to seek another headship?
5   If the time has come to leave headship, should I
    a   seek another post in education?
    or
    b   leave education altogether?

Taking stock in terms of career development is too often undertaken in a state of frustration, weariness or even despair and may be necessitated by poor health. In such conditions, ill-considered decisions and actions are sometimes made. Many teachers, in common with many in other occupations, go through their working lives on a thoroughly pragmatic basis. If the job is agreeable they stay; if it is not, they move. Opportunity plays a considerable part in the job fortunes of an individual. Many are willing and able to respond to it when it comes but they do not particularly seek it.

An alternative is to have a plan at the outset of a teaching career. The majority of teachers know they will be working in four decades of their lives — their 20s, 30s, 40s and 50s. So it is possible to assign targets concerning jobs and salaries at the mid and end points of each of these four decades. In primary education it is possible for a teacher to have a full, exciting and demanding working life for his or her entire professional career. Teachers aspiring to headship want to be effective as Heads. Taking stock in different ways needs to be undertaken in order to be really effective. Taking stock helps the individual towards a greater self-understanding which, above all else, is the bedrock upon which effective management in primary schools depends.

Appendix

DES TWENTY DAY BASIC COURSE IN EDUCATION MANAGEMENT FOR PRIMARY SCHOOL HEADS
(Offered to all Heads in their first five years of Headship)

Course aim

To enhance the management performance of practising primary school Heads in the early years of headship.

Course objectives

The *key objective* for the study and practice of management is to improve the education and welfare of children.

Course members will be enabled to

1. study aspects of school management with a group of fellow Heads using their own schools as the main resource base
2. enrich their understanding of the wider context within which the management of the school is conducted
3. consider policy and practice in financial management
4. update their knowledge of the legal basis for school management
5. increase their understanding and skill in managing human and material resources
6. engage in simulated interviews — selection and appraisal — in order to improve interviewing skills and techniques which are central to staff appointments and staff development
7. review their present school curriculum policy in the light of recent educational developments and government publications
8. consider the bases of team management and team building
9. consider the use of microcomputers and related ancillary equipment
10. examine and evaluate their own management style and managerial performance.

The course

Practical and applied in nature, the course which takes place in four consecutive weeks will give considerable prominence to the case study visits to course members' own schools. These will take place in syndicates of four. The group size will be limited to enable maximum participation to take place in school and in practical activities and discussions on course. Course members will be invited to undertake selective reading, prepare material for the case study visit to their own school and present a curriculum analysis for group discussion.

Tutorial support and access to management literature will be available throughout the course.

Course content

The focus of attention will be on the work of actual schools. Centred on the management interests and responsibilities of primary school Heads, contemporary issues will be highlighted and opportunities offered for conceptual development and skills training.

The course is organised around four main themes:
Theme 1   External relations and material resources
Theme 2   Internal relations and staff development
Theme 3   Management of children and the curriculum
Theme 4   Administration and whole school evaluation

Course sessions

| Session 1 | 9.15–10.30 | Session 3 | 13.30–14.45 |
| Session 2 | 11.00–12.15 | Session 4 | 15.15–16.30 |

Course approach

A variety of approaches will be used. Activities will include the school case study visits and tasks, syndicate meetings, small group work, individual presentations by course members, films, video recordings, simulation and role-playing, intray exercises, talks given by course contributors, reading and plenary discussions.

Between them the course contributors represent a wide range of professional interest and experience in the management of schools. They include experienced primary school Heads, LEA officers, advisers and inspectors, HMI, a senior police officer and educational management consultants.

Course contributors have been briefed to

i)   limit their talk to a *maximum of 40 minutes*
ii)   include activities/tasks for course members to undertake individu-
        ally or in pairs or small groups
iii)   allow ample time for discussion
iv)   distribute a resource paper(s) which relates to the topic
v)   bear in mind that a number of course members are class-teaching
        heads

The Programme

Day 1   Introductory Day (3–4 weeks before Day 2)
            Introductions, Administration and Management Task

Theme 1   *External relations and material resources*

Day 2
1 & 2   The LEA and the school: present and future
3 & 4   Financial management

Day 3
1 & 2   The school and its community — parents and governors
3   School management — a police inspector's perspective
4   Syndicate meetings — preparation for school case study visit

Day 4
            School case study visit (1) — external relations and
            material resources

Day 5
1 & 2   Case study syndicate reports
            Managing external relations & material resources —
            an experienced Head's perspective
3 & 4   Legal aspects of headship

Day 6
1 & 2   Primary headship management issues

Theme 2   *Internal relations and staff development*

Day 6
3 & 4   Staff selection and interviewing

Day 7
1,2 & 3   Staff selection and interviewing (continued) —
            video recording of simulated interviews
4   Syndicate meetings — preparation for school case study visit

Day 8

        School case study visit (2) — internal relations and
        staff development

Day 9

1 & 2   Case study syndicate reports
        Managing internal relations and staff development —
        an experienced Head's perspective
3 & 4   Management style

Day 10

1   The management of time
2,3 & 4 Organisational stress

Day 11

1,2 & 3 Teacher appraisal — staff performance review
4   Teacher appraisal in action — case study of a school

Theme 3   *Management of children and the curriculum*

Day 12

1 & 2   The curriculum — present and future
3   Course members' curriculum presentations
4   Syndicate meetings — preparation for school case study visit

Day 13

        School case study visit (3) — management of children and the
        curriculum

Day 14

1 & 2   Case study syndicate reports
        Managing children and the curriculum — an experienced
        Head's perspective
3 & 4   The management of meetings

Day 15

1   Course administration (45 mins)
1 & 2   Ideas into action
3 & 4   — problem solving in the curriculum

Theme 4   *Administration and whole-school evaluation*

Day 16

1 & 2   Team management
3 & 4   Computers in primary school administration

Day 17
1 & 2   The effective Head — an adviser's perspective
3   Course members' choice
4   Syndicate meetings — preparation for school case study visit

Day 18

School case study visit (4) — administration and
whole-school evaluation

Day 19
1 & 2   Case study syndicate reports
Administration and evaluation — an experienced Head's
perspective
3 & 4   Evaluating schools — an HMI's perspective

Day 20
1 & 2   The Head's managerial performance analysis
3 & 4   Course evaluation

References

1   This study was undertaken by David Picton-Jones, Head of Swanmore CE
    Primary School, Swanmore, Hampshire
2   *The Times Educational Supplement* 15.11.85, p 7
3   *Blackmore Vale Magazine* 28.3.86, p 19
4   Extracted from Paisey, A (1981) 'The Pupil's Experience of School Organi-
    zation' in *School Organization* 1, 3, pp 267–271
5   From *A Rural Headship* (1985) (Unpublished) by Tom Simpson, Head of
    Battle Primary School, Reading
6   Department of Education and Science (1981) *The School Curriculum* Lon-
    don, HMSO, para 11; Department of Education and Science (1985) *The
    Curriculum from 5 to 16 — Curriculum Matters 2* London, HMSO, para 6
7   International Labour Office (1979) *Work Study* Geneva, ILO, pp 101–102
8   Bryant, Sir Arthur (1985) *Pepys — The Years of Peril* London, Panther
    Books, p 144
9   See Croner (1988) *The Head's Legal Guide* New Malden, Croner Publica-
    tions, 1, pp 119–21
10 From an unpublished paper by Lawrence Cameron, former Head of
    Kempshott Junior School, Hampshire, now Senior Lecturer at Bulmershe
    College of Higher Education, Reading
11 From an unpublished paper by Christopher Watts, Head of Northern Parade
    Middle School (8–12), Portsmouth
12 Dorin, P C and Mansergh, G G (1980) 'Middle Management Time Usage'
    in *Catalyst for Change: Journal of the National School Development Council*
    9, 2, pp 4–7 (USA)
13 Morris, V C *et al* (1982) 'The Urban Principal: Middle Manager in the
    Educational Bureaucracy' in *Phi Delta Kappan* 63, 10, pp 689–92 (USA)
14 From an unpublished study by Frank Agness, Head of Loddon Junior School,
    Earley, Reading
15 Harvey, C W (1986) 'How Primary Heads Spend Their Time' in *Educational
    Management and Administration* 14, 1, pp 60–68
16 The terms 'frustration relationship', 'authority relationship' and 'change
    relationship' are taken from Cameron, L G (1984) *An Investigation into the
    Role of the Vice-Principal in Secondary Schools in Northern Ireland* Unpub-
    lished MSc dissertation, University of Ulster.
17 Supplied by Derek Waters, former Head and sometime Director of Inner
    London Education Authority's management training centre for primary
    school staff
18 Adapted from Belbin, R M (1983) *Management Teams: Why they Succeed
    or Fail* London, Heinemann

Selected Further Reading

Books

Belbin, R.M. (1983) *Management Teams: Why They Succeed or Fail* London: Heinemann.

Coulson, A. (1985) 'The managerial behaviour of primary school Heads', *Collected Original Resources in Education* 9, 1.

Craig, I. ed. (1987) *Primary School Management in Action* London: Longman

Croner (1987) *The Head's Legal Guide* New Malden: Croner Publications.

Day, C. Johnston, D. and Whitaker, P. (1986) *Managing Primary Schools: A Professional Development Approach* London: Harper and Row.

Everard, K.B. and Morris, G. (1985) *Effective School Management* Harper and Row.

Everard, K.B. (1986) *Developing Management in Schools* Oxford: Basil Blackwell.

Harling, P. (1984) *New Directions in Educational Leadership* Lewes: The Falmer Press.

Industrial Society (1982–) Management in Schools Series — set of booklets. London: Industrial Society.

Jones, R. (1980) *Primary School Management* Newton Abbott: David and Charles.

Paisey, A. (1981) *Organization and Management in Schools* London: Longman.

Paisey, A. (1984) *School Management — A Case Approach* London: Harper and Row.

Paisey, A. (ed) (1985) *Jobs in Schools — Applying, Interviewing and Selecting for Appointments and Promotions* London: Heinemann.

Rust, W.B. (1985) *Management Guidelines for Teachers* London: Pitman.

Waters, D. (1979) *Management and Headship in the Primary School* London: Ward Lock Educational.

Waters, D. (1983) *Responsibility and Promotion in the Primary School* London: Heinemann.

Whitaker, P. (1983) *The Primary Head* London: Heinemann.

Journals

Educational Management and Administration (Journal of the British Educational Management and Administration Society) Longman.
Education 3–13 (Studies in Education Ltd).
Management in Education (BEMAS) (Harcourt Brace Jovanovich).
School Organization (The Falmer Press).
School Organization and Management Abstracts (Carfax Publishing Company).
Principal (Journal of the National Association of Elementary School Principals, USA). Reston, Virginia.
Review (The National Association of Head Teachers).

Index